T0330692

Rising India

While India's prospects as a rising power and its material position in the international system have received significant attention, little scholarly work exists on India's status in contemporary world politics. This Routledge Focus book charts the ways in which India's international strategies of status seeking have evolved from Independence up to the present day.

The authors focus on the social dimensions of status, seeking to build on recent conceptual scholarship on status in world politics. The book shows how India has made a partial, though incomplete, shift from seeking status by rejecting material power and proximity to major powers, to seeking status by embracing both material power and major power relationships. However, it also challenges traditional understandings of the linear relationship between material power and status. Seven decades of Indian status seeking reveal that the enhancement of material power is one of only several routes Indian leaders have envisaged to lead to higher status.

By arguing that a state requires more than material power to achieve status, this book reshapes understandings of both status seeking and Indian foreign policy. It will be of interest to academics and policy makers in the fields of international relations, foreign policy, and Indian studies.

Rajesh Basrur is Professor of International Relations and Coordinator of the South Asia Programme at RSIS at NTU, Singapore.

Kate Sullivan de Estrada is Lecturer in Modern Indian Studies at the University of Oxford, UK.

Rising India
Status and Power

Rajesh Basrur and Kate Sullivan de Estrada

Routledge
Taylor & Francis Group

LONDON AND NEW YORK

First published 2017
by Routledge
2 Park Square, Milton Park, Abingdon, Oxon OX14 4RN

and by Routledge
711 Third Avenue, New York, NY 10017

Routledge is an imprint of the Taylor & Francis Group, an informa business

© 2017 Rajesh Basrur and Kate Sullivan de Estrada

The right of Rajesh Basrur and Kate Sullivan de Estrada to be identified as authors of this work has been asserted by them in accordance with sections 77 and 78 of the Copyright, Designs and Patents Act 1988.

British Library Cataloguing in Publication Data
A catalogue record for this book is available from the British Library

Library of Congress Cataloging in Publication Data
A catalog record for this book has been requested

ISBN: 978-0-415-78631-7 (hbk)
ISBN: 978-1-31522-782-5 (ebk)

Typeset in Times New Roman
by Taylor & Francis Books

Contents

Preface   vi

1   Strategies of status seeking in world politics: the case of
    India   1

2   Status without power in the Nehru era (1947–1964)   24

3   Incipient power, limited status in the post-Nehru era
    (1964–1991)   54

4   Status and power in the post-Cold War era (1991–2016)   82

5   Conclusion   112

    Bibliography   117
    Index   135

Preface

This book has its origins in a 2012 conversation between the authors on the sidelines of a talk at the Department of Political Science and International Studies, University of Birmingham, hosted by Professor Nick Wheeler. Our shared sense at the time was that there was an interesting story to be told about India's longstanding quest for international status; a story that did not quite mesh with the power-centric analyses which we felt near-dominated the field. Fortuitously, our decision to collaborate on such an account was well timed with the emergence in the discipline of International Relations (IR) of a small but ground-breaking literature on status. In particular, the 2014 edited volume by T. V. Paul, Deborah Welch Larson and William C. Wohlforth, *Status in World Politics*, has been a major source of conceptual inspiration and we owe much to its editors and contributors.

Our own contribution to the emerging scholarship on status through this book fulfils our original aim of narrating one story of India's aspirations to high status in world politics. However, it also offers a conceptual engagement with status-seeking that has application beyond the case of India and that is relevant to the study of other rising powers. While our own thoughts and findings on the subject continue to evolve and far exceed the confines of this slim volume, our aim in writing for the fast-publishing Routledge Focus series is three-fold: to make an early statement on the relationship that India has held with status in world politics; to contribute in a timely manner to the conceptual framing of status in the discipline of IR; and to kindle new and fairly immediate conversations with our colleagues.

We would like to acknowledge the contributions of a number of individuals and institutions in the making of this book. Early papers by the two authors laid its foundation in a small Oxford workshop in March 2015, generously funded by the South Asia Programme, S. Rajaratnam School of International Studies, Nanyang Technological University and hosted by the Contemporary South Asian Studies Programme, Area Studies and the South Asia Research Cluster, Wolfson College, both of the University of Oxford. We would like to thank Professor Yuen Foong Khong and Professor Todd Hall for serving as discussants on the papers, Professor Matthew McCartney for chairing the workshop, Dr George Kunnath for his insightful comments, and Sarah Dewick and Louise Gordon for coordinating the event. In July 2016, an award through the Returning Carer's Fund, Vice-Chancellor's Diversity Fund, University of Oxford, which, among other things, supports career development following maternity leave, permitted the authors to convene once more in Oxford. We thank Stephen Minay for his logistical support in setting up this visit. Perhaps the greatest beneficiaries of both meetings in Oxford were one author's air miles and the other author's two small children, who have learnt to expect the delivery of chocolate from Singapore.

We would like to thank Professor Roy Allison and Dr Gilberto Estrada Harris for their feedback on the introduction, and Padmini Gopal for providing timely assistance with the referencing and bibliography. Finally, we are grateful to Professor Nick Wheeler, both for his perceptive feedback on key parts of the book, and for originally bringing the authors together to learn from one another throughout this exciting project.

1 Strategies of status seeking in world politics

The case of India

Introduction

While India's prospects as a rising power and its material position in the international system have received significant attention,[1] little scholarly work exists on India's *status* in contemporary world politics.[2] Given the broad scholarly consensus that 'India's evolution into a modern nation state has been marked by an inordinate quest for international recognition of its status', it is surprising how little theorising and empirical analysis of India's status seeking has taken place.[3] Since Independence, India's leaders have consistently sought high international status for the Indian state, even if the strategies they have adopted have shifted over time. Independent India's first prime minister, Jawaharlal Nehru, firmly believed that India was a 'potential Great Power'.[4] Half a century after his passing, there is a widespread sense that this potential is close to being realised. The combination of economic growth, rising military power and revived recognition as the 'world's greatest democracy' has fostered a returning consciousness among Indian elites of their country's past greatness and future destiny as a major power.[5] As Prime Minister Narendra Modi told a news channel in September 2014, 'This is a country that once upon a time was called "the golden bird". We have fallen from where we were before. But now we have the chance to rise again'.[6] The ubiquitous sense of national pride visible today has an old lineage. The eleventh-century traveller and diarist Alberuni had observed: 'the Indians believe that there is no country but theirs, no king like theirs, no religion like theirs, no science like theirs'.[7]

The purpose of this volume is to offer a fresh interpretation of India's now seven decades-old search for higher status. In order to do so, it draws on – and advances – recent International Relations (IR) scholarship on status seeking that underscores not simply the material but also the social dimensions of status in world politics.

We define status as 'the condition of filling a place in a social hier-archy', in the present case the states system.[8] At heart, status conveys a sense of rank or standing and is essentially hierarchical. It is close to, but encompasses more than the concept of prestige,[9] which in turn denotes authority – an attribute that is important in determining a state's ability to exercise influence while minimising costs.[10] Other related concepts include recognition, honour and esteem.[11]

The realist tradition in IR implies a linear relationship between material power and status, anticipating that as a state's material power increases, so will its status.[12] At first glance, India's status-seeking experience appears to conform with this relationship. During the early post-independence decades, India's status was limited by its material weakness; in recent years, its material growth has propelled its rising international status. But, as we will show, the reality is more complex than the picture drawn by realists. First, India was able during the initial years to craft a strategy that gave it a level of status that exceeded typical realist expectations, despite its economic and military weakness. This strategy was based not only on India's potential for material growth, but perhaps even more on two other factors that were normative: its use of ideational power – in attempting to set a post-colonial global agenda – as a substitute for material strength; and its domestic poli-tical institutions, which gave it the claim of being the world's largest democracy.

This early pattern of India's status-seeking behaviour contrasts markedly with the post-Cold War period, where India has experienced rapid economic growth, declared a nuclear weapons capability, and become the world's largest importer of arms. In many ways, India appears to have shifted from seeking status by rejecting material power and proximity to major powers, to seeking status by embracing both material power and major power relationships. But even here, as we will show, India's ability to project itself as a 'responsible' power has helped it greatly in obtaining status accommodation as a rising power.

The account presented in this short volume contests the realist reading of India's record of status seeking. We see India's apparent shift from status seeking on the basis of non-material power to status seeking through material power as partial and much more nuanced than is commonly understood. We also identify a number of puzzling moments that do not appear to fit with the established linear perspective. The realist understanding of material power as the central foundation for status cannot explain why early Indian governments deprioritised India's military development and engaged in efforts to challenge material capability as a central criterion for status in international politics. India's nuclear history is equally puzzling: why, when India could have tested nuclear weapons as early as 1965, did Indian representatives seek to delink prestige from nuclear weapons in global negotiating forums up until the late 1980s?[13] Why did Indira Gandhi take the decision to conduct a nuclear test in 1974, but not move towards the nuclear weaponisation of the Indian state? Finally, why has post-Cold War India, despite the rapid rise in its military power, resisted power projection and eschewed intervening, in the latter case sometimes – as with Sri Lanka in the mid-2000s and Iraq in 2003 – even when invited to do so?

Our contention in this book is that India's status-seeking strategies since Independence do not project an easy or straightforward relationship with material power. By focussing on the *social* dimensions of status in world politics, in tandem with the traditional emphasis on material dimensions, our analysis sheds light on many of these questions, and delivers a nuanced account of India's post-Independence quest for higher status that challenges traditional understandings of the linear relationship between material power and status. Moreover, it also offers important insights into India's future as a rising power. India's efforts to enhance its material power are not particularly recent, nor wholesale, nor are they the only route Indian leaders have envisaged to lead to high status.

The research question

In this study, we seek to address the following research question: in the history of India's post-Independence quest for higher status in world politics, what is the relationship between material power and status seeking? The question is by no means easy to answer. The expansion of economic and military power (aimed at enhancing security) gives rise more often than not to higher status, though not necessarily so. But independent India under Prime Minister Jawaharlal Nehru began its quest for status without directly seeking material power. Subsequently, under his successors and until the end of the 1990s, India sought material power, essentially for security purposes, and continued its previous quest for status on a non-material basis. After 1991, there has been a confluence of the two objectives: India has pursued material power for both security and status, though a significant (some would say excessive) proportion of its diplomatic efforts has focused – we shall show – on attaining status objectives.

Situating the study: understandings of status in world politics

A standard approach to differentiating states – usually adopted by realists – is to classify them according to their capabilities, for example, as a superpower, great power, major power, or minor power.[14] Such classificatory systems tend to be based primarily on hard power resources. They therefore leave little space to understand India as a state that has sought status on the basis of some degree of normative influence throughout its independent history. We also consider it important to differentiate between status as viewed by analysts and status as accorded by policy makers – the two may not coincide. Below, we engage with the existing scholarship on status in IR and beyond, and take a position on the chief material and ideational components of status. We then move on to present our own definition for the purposes of this study.

Determinants of status – I: material power sources

Scholars of status who – in line with the realist approach we refer to above – assume a logical progression from rising material power resources to the attainment of higher status, tend to place primary focus on the military and economic attributes of states.[15] Others hold that domestic constraints prevent a state from acquiring higher status.[16] We view two dimensions of material capabilities as contributing to status: (i) economic and military capacity; and (ii) links with major powers. But while there is a close relationship between material power and status, it is not a unilineal one. For instance, states may seek and obtain higher status based on some non-material capabilities, for example middle powers such as Australia and Canada.[17] Small powers like Norway may also achieve relatively high status unconnected with their material capabilities.[18]

Determinants of status – II: normative sources

Recent scholarship on status in world politics distinguishes between a state's social status and its material position within the international system.[19] Deborah Welch Larson, T. V. Paul and William C. Wohlforth in the introduction to their volume on *Status in World Politics* define status as 'collective beliefs about a given state's ranking on valued attributes'.[20] They posit that status is evaluated on the basis of attributes, some of which 'are measurable – such as the size of the national economy or military forces' and others which are 'more intangible assets such as cultural achievement, soft power, and moral authority'.[21] In all cases, the attributes must be collectively valued, or, at least, valued by dominant states. In other words, status is determined in a social context, where that context is structured by power relations of different kinds.

Significantly, it matters whether a state is in tune with dominant systemic norms and values. For instance, Yong Deng shows how China has had difficulties in attaining respect and esteem as a major power because it does not fit into the prevailing value system primarily shaped by the major powers, owing to its non-democratic internal politics.[22] As will be seen, India, for all its flaws, has done much better in obtaining widespread recognition as a democratic state.

Less widely enunciated but nevertheless important is the contemporary notion of a 'good power', whose behaviour displays 'good international citizenship', encompassing enlightened national interest as well as a commitment to 'community values'.[23] Norway has been widely acknowledged for its contributions to global stability (in the Middle East, Bosnia, Sri Lanka and elsewhere).[24] British and Japanese efforts to present themselves as 'good states' may also be seen as status-seeking behaviours. Japan wrote off developing-country debt at substantial cost to itself in 1999 and ratified the Kyoto Protocol in 2003 despite the potential costs and US opposition to the agreement. The UK supported the establishment of the International Criminal Court despite the risk of incurring costs to itself and opposition to the ICC from the US.[25]

If we view status as determined through conformity to dominant systemic norms and values, and understand that norms also socially regulate the material realm, we can come to a different understanding of the material attributes of status that preoccupy realists. Richard Ned Lebow points to international social consensus over the status-enhancing role of military power in contemporary international society.[26] In this view, material and economic power are crucial status determinants because they are dominantly, socially recognised as valuable – a reading that differs from an understanding of the significance of material power solely as security-enhancing.

Murray Milner's general theory of status relationships (based on his study of status in the Indian caste system) differentiates between sources of status that are *associational* (that is, based on the possession of material assets or proximity to other, high-status actors) and those that are *normative* (that is, largely based on conformity with dominant social norms).[27] Milner views *associations* with particular, intersubjectively-valued objects and actors – essentially, material attributes and relationships – as an important source of status.[28] In world politics, we see that associations with highly-valued material assets and with other high status or powerful actors are central to the attainment of high status – but only because there is social consensus regarding their value.

Readings of the normative sources of status view conformity with dominant systemic norms as the primary route to status. However, as we explore below in relation to status-seeking strategies, under rare conditions, innovation with regard to dominant systemic norms can also deliver status.

As we see it, India has sought, like numerous other states, to stress its claims to higher status on the basis of not only its material resources, but also its being a 'good power' (without using the precise term). In contrast with China, India has been able to enjoy a relatively smooth path to higher status because of (a) its largely successful effort to project itself as a vibrant (though in numerous ways non-mature) democracy; and (b) its claim to be a 'responsible' power (akin to the notion of a 'good state'), which combines military restraint with contribution to the public good. Together, these have contributed to a positive image that has been utilised to justify its aspirations to enter the United Nations Security Council (UNSC) and the Nuclear Suppliers Group (NSG).

We also consider India's associations with material assets, such as conventional military forces and (more problematically) nuclear weapons, and with high-status states, such as the United States, as key determinants of its social status, because dominant systemic norms attach value to these assets and actors. In addition, India has tried to be creative in demonstrating its commitment to norms by emphasising its character as a 'responsible' power.

Determinants of status – III: status accommodation

Ultimately, a state attains higher status only if those already at a higher level acknowledge the aspirant as being at their own level.[29] This can take the form of including the aspirant in elite clubs such as the UNSC or the G7/G8. The study of the US response to India's rise shows that status accommodation is in the process of occurring. Major indicators are the acceptance (in principle) by most major powers of India's claim to permanent membership of the UNSC; and the US willingness to push for an India-specific exemption to the rules of the NSG and its own domestic law in order to allow India to trade in nuclear materials.

Status accommodation is a useful concept in comprehending a state's status-seeking strategies and experience. First, the amenability of a higher-level state to accommodating an aspiring state facilitates the latter's efforts to climb up the social hierarchy. Accommodation may also be partial or incomplete, as in the case of China, as noted by Yong Deng above. Second, a major determinant of the established state's willingness to confer higher status on the aspiring state is the former's strategic interest at any point of time. Status may be accorded *before* a state acquires actual material power, as when China was accorded higher status by the United States in the 1940s and again in the 1970s.[30] Third, if the aspiring state's strategic behaviour is in tune with the strategic interests of the established/dominant state(s), the former's task becomes that much easier. This is clear if we contrast India–US relations during the Nehru era, when India's grand strategy was tangential to that of the US, with relations in the post-Cold War years, when New Delhi's strategic preferences have been much more in tune with those of Washington.

Status consistency/inconsistency

Status consistency/inconsistency refers to the match/mismatch between a state's aspirations to higher status and the response it receives from higher-ranked states. Baldev Raj Nayar and T. V. Paul describe 'status inconsistency' as the discrepancy between a state's capabilities and aspirations on the one hand and its ascribed status on the other.[31] Whereas they treat India as a status-inconsistent state, Rajesh Basrur treats it as a status consistent state, that is, its status is more or less on par with its (relatively limited) capabilities.[32] Our analysis does not dwell on the question of consistency, though we do recognise that there is a strong motivation to push for status where Indian elites view it as being denied, for example, on India's membership of institutions of the non-proliferation regime (the Nuclear Non-Proliferation Treaty, or NPT, excepted). Our focus is primarily on the analysis of status-seeking *strategy*.

Status-seeking strategies

The status-seeking strategies of states have been analysed in different ways. Richard Ned Lebow has classified such strategies as (1) *emulation* or association with (a) the material attributes of great powers; and (b) specific great powers by way of balance-of-power or like behaviour (alliance making; partnership building); (2) *deviance* or violating the norms of the system to gain attention and recognition; and (3) *challenge* or attempting to change the rules governing how honour and office are conferred, or even developing alternative hierarchies.[33] Deborah Welch Larson and Alexei Shevchenko's three strategies are slightly different: (1) *emulation* – emulating the values and practices of great powers; (2) *competition* – attempting to equal or surpass the great powers in areas on which their claim to high status rests; and (3) *creativity* – stressing an unconventional attribute or approach that it claims makes it worthy of higher status.[34] Rohan Mukherjee categorises status-seeking strategies as *rule taking* – adhering to existing norms and institutions; *rule breaking* – challenging the existing order, primarily for effect; and *rule shaping* – contributing in partnership with others to emerging norms and building nascent regimes.[35] We prefer a simpler classification that subsumes all of the above. We hold that there are primarily two strategies that status-seeking states use:

a   *conformity*, which includes emulation, but may also encompass competition as well as degrees of innovation within the existing framework; and
b   *rejection*, which includes either (a) violation of existing systemic rules/norms; and/or (b) creativity, which involves efforts to generate alternative rules/norms.

Status as a power resource

Status is both an end – a social good – and a means – an instrument to achieve other ends. Geoffrey Brennan and Philip Pettit's work on esteem holds analytical insights that are useful for an understanding of status. Esteem is sought and desired 'for a mix of pragmatic and evidentiary reasons', that is, 'it clearly helps us attain other goods and makes it easier to think well of ourselves'.[36] Status seeking may equally be considered as having pragmatic and evidentiary aims. The two may not always be distinguishable.

Status can serve as a resource for influencing the behaviour of other actors. It is not always easy to clearly distinguish the motivations of status seeking from power seeking since both can manifest as an instrumental approach to the conduct of social relations.[37] Status can be seen to work instrumentally in a number of ways. Robert Keohane, for example, suggests that the outcome of a state's effort to increase its external esteem may include the attraction of foreign investment and other economic benefits.[38] A state with high status may therefore become a preferred trading partner or political ally and thus derive material benefit from its high status in the eyes of other states. Apart from the benefits that accrue from outside, an increase in status can result in heightened domestic support for those at the helm of a state and thus function as an internal source of power.[39]

While it is not possible here to comprehensively explore the role that status plays in determining the outcomes of social relations, the important point to note is that status *can* be an autonomous domain to material power, and that benefits can be derived from status that do not require the direct exercise of power to coerce or induce. As the early history of India's status seeking shows, achieving high status can be a priority for a state which de-prioritises the use of coercive power in its conduct with other states.

Further, the close interaction of a status-seeking state with other entities can create 'social capital', which may be described as 'the aggregate of the actual or potential resources which are linked to possession of a durable network of more or less institutionalised relationships of mutual acquaintance or recognition'.[40] The key benefits of networking include inflow of useful information, mutual aid through bridging and bonding, enhanced scope for collective action, and the forming of solidarity among network members.[41] More specifically, evidence from diverse fields such as international political economy, security, local politics and sociology points to the advantages that can be derived from networking in terms of gaining influence and upward mobility, and the role that status itself can play in fostering such networks.[42]

Studies of India and status

To date, there is only one substantial work that touches on the issue of status with respect to India's foreign relations: Baldev Raj Nayar and T. V. Paul's 2003 book, *India in the World Order: Searching for Major Power Status* (Cambridge: Cambridge University Press, 2003). As an early contribution to the status literature, this is a significant volume. However, it has certain shortcomings that limit its value today. First, the book's authors have relatively little to say about the concept of status (which they never clearly define), whereas our study builds upon and refines the concept on the basis of the considerable work done in the last decade. Second, the analysis is confined primarily to the issue of 'status inconsistency', that is, it focuses mainly on the systemic constraints on India's rise to major power status rather than on India's status-seeking strategies. Third, Nayar and Paul overwhelmingly equate status with material power, whereas we show that, while there is much overlap between the two, there is also a significant distinction between them. Important elements of Indian strategic behaviour can only be understood in the light of this distinction. Fourth, Nayar and

Paul's account does not fully recognise the alternative pathways to higher status taken by India, a point that is central to our study. Fifth, their study also misses the sharp difference we stress between India's status-seeking strategy in the global and regional contexts during the Cold War era and the more recent move toward congruence between these realms. Finally, the Nayar and Paul volume is in important respects outdated because India has begun to build close strategic relationships with the United States and Japan and has embarked on a massive military modernisation programme, both of which occurred after the period covered in their account.

Beyond Nayar and Paul's work, there are several recent works that either focus on India as a rising power or offer an account of transitions in India's foreign policy.[43] However, no work to date has offered a comprehensive account of India's status-seeking strategies in world politics.

Defining status: theoretical assumptions

Building upon the above literature on status in world politics, the starting point of our analysis is the wide consensus that a state's status is socially constructed. Rather than following automatically from the distribution of material capabilities, status is 'contingent on socially constructed standards of belonging that are normative, not just material'.[44] Status is therefore a social relationship and implies the existence of a social hierarchy.[45] As Larson et al. note, '[w]hich states occupy a higher position than others is not an environmental attribute independent of perception and observable by all; it is a social construction'.[46]

Status seeking among and within groups of states thus takes place within a specific social and historical context.[47] As Milner notes, 'general societal norms tend to be associated with the interests of dominant groups'; thus status in the society of states as a whole tends to be determined by the great powers at any given time. Material power is highly valued and constitutes the primary qualification for status in a system or society of states (and we use these terms interchangeably)[48] that has been frequently defined through the existence of anarchy or the absence of a higher sovereign authority over states. Over the past century and more, capitalism, too, has enjoyed high standing and, since the end of the Cold War, has been embraced by all of the major powers. Dominant states are usually also the states with the highest status, and they typically function as the key actors in status accommodation (the recognition or conferral of status).

In order to bring greater analytical clarity to the question of the sources of status, we draw on Milner's theory of status relationships to differentiate between determinants of status that are (1) *associational*, that is, (a) based on the possession of material assets that are dominantly, socially valued, and/or (b) based on proximity to dominant, high-status actors; and (2) *normative*, that is, largely based on conformity with dominant social/systemic norms.

Associations with intersubjectively valued objects and actors – essentially, material attributes and relationships – are an important source of status.[49] In contemporary world politics, we see that associations with highly valued material assets and with other high-status or dominant actors, in particular the United States, remain central to high status. Material power is status enhancing because it is dominantly, socially recognised as such. Indeed, Lebow argues that military power continues to be intersubjectively accepted as 'the principal criterion for ranking states' within the world community.[50] This means that while material power is significant to states because it is security-enhancing, it is also significant as a determinant of a state's social status. Proximity to dominant, high-status actors and conformity to their interests is also status-enhancing. However, dominant, high-status actors can also present a barrier to status: as Milner notes, status is 'a relatively inexpansible resource; therefore, those with high status have both the motivation and the ability to restrict and regulate mobility'.[51]

Normative sources of status largely manifest as conformity, resistance/ deviance or innovation vis-à-vis the prevailing dominant social/systemic norms – though these may be contested[52] – in the world order. Positive status typically results from the approval received for conformity to dominant norms, such as India's post-Cold War conformity to the dominant idea of legitimate statehood: liberal democracy.[53] Conformity with dominant social/systemic norms is a crucial status determinant because such norms are typically formulated by dominant, high-status states (the central actors in status accommodation) to both serve their interests and (to a lesser extent) to project their identities and values. Negative status can result from deviance from dominant norms, for example, when India violated a key non-proliferation norm (and emerging non-testing norm) by testing nuclear weapons in 1998. As Milner notes, however, the 'highest levels of status are sometimes associated with innovation', thus innovative behaviours in relation to dominant social/ systemic norms can also serve as sources of status.[54] India saw status gains in the early decades after independence in part due to innovation, when Indian leaders were proactive in formulating and shaping elements of a counter-order within both the United Nations and through the Non-Aligned Movement (NAM), but this status was conferred less by the dominant powers than by the followers India cultivated among weaker states. Envisioning status as socially constructed implies, of course, an audience. Leadership, enacted through the formulation of new norms, or through the innovation around existing ones, needs to be accepted by followers.[55]

While our definition of status along the above lines does not assume covariation between material power and social status, we do, however, see them as related in two important ways. First, as we note in relation to the associational determinants of status, we can expect a state to seek status on the basis of military and economic power because these assets are dominantly recognised as status enhancing in the international environment. Second, states also require material capability to 'act in accord with certain socially constructed procedures and standards required of the desired status', something that Clunan describes as 'status enactment'.[56] We consider status enactment to overlap in an important way with the concept of responsibility in world politics. While one conception of responsibility envisages responsible status to follow through a state's conformity to dominant norms (responsibility 'from below'),[57] as described above, another conception centres on the role of dominant powers in upholding the global order through the securing of conformity from other states (responsibility 'from above'),[58] a role that typically requires significant power resources.

A state's material power may therefore enhance its status because material power is socially valued, or a state may require (and acquire) material capability in order that it may enact its status.

Understanding India's status-seeking strategies: methodological approach

As the framing of our research question makes clear, this study aims to explore the relationship between material power and status seeking within the context of a single case study, that of India. However, we see India as one of a broader category of states currently seeking high status in world politics, including China, Brazil, Japan, Russia and South Africa. In this sense, we accept John Gerring's definition of a case study as 'an intensive study of a single unit for the purpose of understanding a larger class of (similar) units'.[59] In other words, while our focus is the relationship between material power and status in India's status-seeking strategies, we are equally interested in drawing out observations and patterns that are pertinent to other rising states.

At the same time, since our definition of status is inherently social, and since we posit status-seeking states as functioning within and responding to a social order, our study is not simply an examination of a repertoire of status-seeking strategies available to and utilised by states, but also an (albeit far more limited) explication of the (shifting) social context in which states have sought high international status over the past seventy years of India's independent history. In this vein, we draw inspiration from Michael Burawoy's 'extended case method', which posits that the ability to generalise from a single case rests on 'what it tells us about the world in which it is embedded'.[60] Burawoy's method aims to uncover how 'micro situations are shaped by wider structures' and, as such, '[t]he importance of the single case lies in what it can tell us about society as a whole'.[61] Accordingly, we treat the evolving international social order as a central (though not the sole) determinant of India's shifting patterns of status seeking in world politics.

In order to draw out these two sets of insights – the status-seeking strategies of states and the evolution of the social context within which they deploy these strategies – we structure our analysis across three periods in independent India's history, therefore eliciting temporal variation in both India's status-seeking strategies and in the dominant systemic norms that typically determine the sources of status. Two of our three chronological phases map onto key turning points in India's history of international engagement. The first spans the period 1947–1964, a period we term the 'Nehru era', when India's status-seeking strategies were largely under the leadership of India's first prime and foreign minister Jawaharlal Nehru, prior to his death in 1964. The second spans the period 1964–1991, a period we refer to as the 'post-Nehru era', during which time Indian leaders were seeking to compensate for some of the failings of the Nehru era, in particular, resistance to the acquisition of material power. The third, the period from 1991 to the present, is the widely acknowledged post-Cold War era, a phase of seismic transition for both the world order and India alike.

We consider the temporal structuring of our analysis to be central to drawing out the changing relationship between material power and status seeking in India's strategy. In each period, we show how India's orientation toward associational and normative aspects of status seeking undergoes distinctive shifts and we discuss some of the elements of the 'wider structures' that make India's status-seeking strategies either meaningful or prone to failure in each period.

In terms of the associational sources of status, we assume that dominant systemic norms within world politics determine that material power, close associations with dominant states (where these states vary across the three periods), and alignment with the interests of dominant states remain status-enhancing across India's independent history. Thus, across the three time periods, we examine India's relationship with conventional military and nuclear capabilities and the prevailing dominant power/s and their interests.

During the Nehru era, dominant systemic norms included power politics, which underscored the 'right' versus the 'wrong' side of global political divisions and rivalry; and liberal democracy and capitalism (challenged by socialism/communism). India rejected power politics and stood for liberal democracy, but not the established forms of capitalist or socialist economics. In the post-Nehru era, power politics and capitalism/socialism remained dominant and were supplemented by the emerging norm of nuclear non-proliferation. India remained opposed to global power politics, but not to power politics in its own region; continued to resist capitalism; was uncertain in its commitment to democracy; and challenged the newly developing non-proliferation regime centred on the NPT. In the post-Cold War period, power politics has remained in place, capitalism has emerged unchallenged; the democracy norm has been strengthened (though with major challenges emerging in China and Russia), and non-proliferation has remained a powerful norm despite significant vulnerabilities. India has, on the whole, drawn much closer to these dominant norms. It has rapidly modernised its military as a 'rising power', embraced capitalism and performed well in terms of economic growth, shown a degree of democratic maturing, and – notwithstanding its challenge to the NPT by way of the 1998 tests – has adhered to non-proliferation norms, including those enshrined in the NPT.[62] These norms include a moratorium on further testing and control over the export of nuclear weapons-related material and technology. In addition, it has sought to don the mantle of a 'responsible' power and demonstrate a strong commitment to the stability of the states system by exercising military restraint and projecting what might be called the 'soft face' of its rising military power.

A central challenge in examining India's status-seeking strategies is the act of identifying status-seeking behaviours. It is not always possible to determine, for example, whether certain behaviours are aimed at enhancing status, or at something else. It is especially difficult to distinguish between security-seeking and status-seeking behaviours since both often involve the pursuit of material power. Such ambiguities can perhaps never completely be overcome; however we draw on a combination of three methods of reading status seeking into given behaviours. First, as already noted, we consider India's behaviours in relation to dominant normative understandings of status. We assume the pursuit of behaviours of conformity (as well as successful cases of innovation) in relation to dominant normative understandings to be status-*enhancing*. Second, to determine whether behaviours are status-*seeking*, we examine, in particular, behaviours that entail significant diplomatic effort but do not seem to deliver significant material rewards, such as India's early investment in and leadership of the NAM and its more recent activism to secure membership of the NSG. Third, we look for evidence of status ambitions in the accounts that leaders themselves offer of their behaviours. For example, when Prime Minister Modi declares before a domestic audience, in relation to India's bid for a permanent seat on the UN Security Council, that 'nobody is paying attention to our contribution [to peace and security]', we infer a status concern.[63] Ultimately, identifying status-seeking behaviours is a matter of interpretation, and we seek to offer plausible evidence[64] wherever possible.

We draw on three key types of evidentiary material in order to empirically furnish our analysis. First, we engage with existing histories and studies, but expand and reinterpret these narratives through the application of our analytical framework of associational and normative status, outlined above. Second, we make use of primary sources, such as speeches and official documents, in order to verify and bolster the secondary material where required for our status analysis. Third, in order to identify behaviours that fit with our understanding of status seeking, we consult memoirs, oral histories and other non-official or domestic 'texts', such as speeches before domestic audiences, and (in more recent times) public interviews and televised debates. We engage interpretively with the latter sources, particularly ones that deliver a sense of status ambition. We argue that interviews with Indian leaders and foreign policy elites are less helpful for identifying India's quest for status because actors are often reluctant to admit or do not recognise their actions and decisions as status motivated. This may be particularly so in the Indian context, where historically, leaders and foreign policy elites, with some exceptions, have been reluctant to openly admit that India is seeking power and status.[65]

Argument and overview of the book

The structure of this book follows our broad periodisation of India's status-seeking strategies into three periods – Chapter 2: the Nehru era (1947–1964), Chapter 3: the post-Nehru era (1964–1991) and Chapter 4: the post-Cold War era (1991–2016). Our central argument is that, contrary to assumptions of a linear relationship between material power and status, the relationship between material power and status as manifested in independent India's engagement in world politics is more complex. Indeed, India's status seeking had some success in the absence of material power, and India has required more than simply material power in order to achieve high status.

In Chapter 2, we show how India attempted to achieve higher status during the Nehru era without focusing strongly on the associational sources of status, namely material power (and especially military power) and alliance relationships with either of the dominant states of the time, the United States and the Soviet Union. Instead, India's status-seeking efforts took the form of 'counter-order' efforts, and centred on innovation with regard to the dominant norms of the system. They involved assuming a leadership role in an effort to craft a transformation of the two chief characteristics of the global system: the Cold War and the capitalist world economy. The diffusion of the confrontation between East and West would create a militarily more secure world; the restructuring of North–South relations a more egalitarian, economically secure, and welfare-maximising one. This approach sought to build status without material power and aimed, in the long run, to utilise higher status to reconstruct the world for the achievement of greater security as well as other values.

In Chapter 3, we argue that this world view collapsed when India lost its war with China in 1962. Thereafter, the primary focus from 1964 to 1991 shifted to building national security through material, especially military, power and simultaneously attempting to remake the world as before. The lesson learned was that status seeking on the basis of innovation cannot be achieved without a material basis. Not only did India rapidly build military power, but it also exercised this power forcefully through interventions that gave it the reputation of a regional policeman. This appeared to confirm the realist axiom that material power must underpin a quest for status. Yet important elements of the earlier approach remained: India continued its attempts to transform the strategic and economic structures of the world and to reject nuclear weapons despite having carried out a test in 1974. Thus, the quest for status through innovation with regard to the dominant norms of the system continued in parallel with the pursuit of material power as a means to security.

In Chapter 4, we document how, after 1991, the twin processes of building material power and pursuing status have continued. The associational determinants of status, such as India's accelerated economic growth and military build-up, have given India the status of a 'rising power'. But simultaneously, India has sought to bolster its claim to higher status by means of conformity with a number of dominant system norms designed to bring it status as a 'responsible' power. In this contemporary period, the associational sources of status – material power and a close relationship with the dominant power in this period, the United States – are primary, but they are not enough to confer status on a state; it matters too what a state *does* with its power, that is, its capacity to conform with status-enactment norms through contributions to a stable world order and/or public goods. India has sought not only to acquire the associational attributes of status through the instruments of military power, but also to bolster its normative claims to status by exercising military restraint, utilising its military capacity for the public good (such as anti-piracy, disaster relief, and search and rescue missions), adhering to evolving systemic norms such as nonproliferation and, more generally, highlighting its democratic political practice to underline its outlook as a benign power. In part, this seems to be in accord with the realist perspective. But it also reflects the changing ethos of the system, which is moving slowly toward a conception of status that goes beyond the possession and exercise of power. In addition, India's strong emphasis (in practice rather than merely in words) on the non-application of force and its resistance to status enactment through securing normative compliance from other states brings to its status claims a distinctiveness that again sets it apart from realist claims.

Key contributions and significance of the study

In presenting our account of India's status-seeking strategies from Independence to the present day, we make three contributions to the literature on status in world politics.

First, realists and other theorists of status position material power as a prerequisite of status. Once states acquire power, they can claim status, though they may or may not attain it since an aspirant's status has to be conferred by higher-status states, that is, through accommodation. This relates to being in conformity with dominant norms established by dominant states. We note, however, that the Indian case is different: India under Nehru sought status through an innovative strategy *before* acquiring power. This did work for some time – India, so to say, punched above its very limited weight for the better part of the Nehru era. Eventually the strategy failed, however, as India lost status following its 1962 defeat. Our understanding of material power as a socially constructed status determinant allows us to understand these puzzling elements of India's relationship with material power. We show how India's early attempts to seek status in the absence of material power in part can be seen as acts of normative innovation, intended to detach value from the possession of material power. We note that these strategies of status seeking ultimately failed, but we also show how some elements have seen short-lived and longer-term successes.

Second, the status literature recognises that states may seek a creative or innovative strategy, but there is no convincing analysis demonstrating the value or success of such a strategy. Neither China nor Russia have been able to draw much advantage from demonstrating 'responsibility' because their fundamental domestic institutional arrangements are not in tune with US-shaped systemic norms such as democracy and human rights, and both have retreated from an image as a responsible power through their actions and attitude vis-à-vis the South and East China Seas and Eastern Europe, respectively. In contrast, India has accelerated its acquisition of material power but seems no closer to projecting that power. In fact, India's growing possession of material power can be viewed as status enhancing, in part because it is not deployed in ways that impinge negatively upon the dominant social/systemic norms that structure the current world order. India's early, large-scale innovative behaviours, such as its counter-order challenges mounted through the NAM, enjoyed limited long-term success. One of India's more recent innovative strategies, its claims to responsible status as a nuclear-armed state outside the NPT, has achieved success only because it status as a non-NPT signatory has come to be seen as an ultimately quite minor normative deviation, given India's broad compliance with much of the NPT regime.

Third, and in sum, our analytical distinction between the associational and normative sources of status captures both the material and non-material sources of status in world politics. In short, we argue that an aspirant state is most likely to be granted higher status if (i) it has the prerequisite associational attributes (material power and links to the major powers and their interests); and (ii) it is in conformity, or predominantly in conformity, with the norms established by the dominant power(s). Our reading of the significance of a state's conformity with dominant systemic norms as a source of status allows us to understand how a state requires more than simply material power in order to acquire high status. India's levels of material power are lower than those of Russia and China but, in contrast, India has been able to a significant degree to attain higher status because its domestic political system as well as its external behaviour have been largely consistent with dominant social norms.

Notes

1 For an optimistic view, though most see India as having some time to go before it can be seen as having 'arrived' as a major power, see Baru,

Sanjaya, *Strategic Consequences of India's Economic Performance* (New Delhi: Academic Foundation, 2006); Curtis, Lisa, 'India's Expanding Role in Asia: Adapting to Rising Power Status', *Backgrounder*, no. 2008, Heritage Foundation, 20 February 2007; Paul, T. V., and Mahesh Shankar, 'Status Accommodation through Institutional Means: India's Rise in the Global Order', in T. V. Paul, Deborah Welch Larson and William C. Wohlforth, eds, *Status in World Politics* (New York: Cambridge University Press, 2014), pp. 165–191. For cautionary views, see Ganguly, Sumit, 'Think Again: India's Rise', *Foreign Policy* (5 July 2012), www.foreignpolicy.com/a rticles/2012/07/05/think_again_india_s_rise (accessed on 6 December 2016); Gordon, Sandy, *India's Rise as an Asian Power: Nation, Neighbourhood, and Region* (Washington, DC: Georgetown University Press, 2014); Malone, David M., *Does the Elephant Dance? Contemporary Indian Foreign Policy* (Oxford: Oxford University Press, 2011); Narlikar, Amrita, 'All that Glitters Is Not Gold: India's Rise to Power', *Third World Quarterly*, vol. 28, no. 5 (2007), pp. 983–996; Volgy, Thomas J., Renato Corbetta, J. Patrick Rhamey Jr, Ryan G. Baird and Keith A. Grant, 'Status Considerations in International Politics and the Rise of Regional Powers', in Paul et al., *Status in World Politics*, pp. 58–84.

2 Basrur, Rajesh, 'India: A Major Power in the Making', in Thomas J. Volgy, Renato Corbetta, Keith A. Grant and Ryan G. Baird, eds, *Major Powers and the Quest for Status in International Politics* (New York: Palgrave Macmillan, 2011); Nayar, Baldev Raj and T. V. Paul, *India in the World Order: Searching for Major Power Status* (Cambridge: Cambridge University Press, 2003); Paul, T. V. and Mahesh Shankar, 'Status Accommodation through Institutional Means', in Paul et al., *Status in World Politics*, pp. 165–191.

3 Mehta, Pratap Bhanu, 'Still Under Nehru's Shadow? The Absence of Foreign Policy Frameworks in India', *India Review*, vol. 8, no. 3 (2009), pp. 209–233, p. 217. See also, for instance: Cohen, Stephen P., *India: Emerging Power* (Washington, DC: Brookings Institution Press, 2001); Amrita Narlikar, 'Peculiar Chauvinism or Strategic Calculation? Explaining the Negotiating Strategy of a Rising India', *International Affairs*, vol. 82, no. 1 (2006), pp. 59–76; Pardesi, Manjeet S., 'Understanding the Rise of India', *India Review*, vol. 6, no. 3 (2007), pp. 209–231.

4 Nayar and Paul, *India in the World Order*, p. 133.

5 Cohen, *India: Emerging Power*.

6 'Modi: India Can Rise Again', *The Hindu*, 22 September 2014, www.the hindu.com/news/national/modi-india-can-rise-again-as-global-power/a rticle6432851.ece (Unless otherwise indicated, all news citations were accessed on the same day as their publication.)

7 Alberuni, cited in: Cohen, *India: Emerging Power*, p. 51.

8 Neumann, Iver B., and Benjamin de Carvalho, 'Introduction: Small States and Status', in Benjamin de Carvalho and Iver B. Neumann, eds, *A Great Power Performance: Norway's Quest for Higher Standing* (Abingdon and New York: Routledge, 2015), pp. 56–72.

9 For Hans Morgenthau, the purpose of a policy of prestige is 'to impress other nations with the power one's own nation actually possesses, or the power it believes, or wants the other nations to believe, it possesses'. His argument is that prestige must draw on forms of power that are recognised

by other states, that is, 'military strength … the most obvious measure of a nation's power'. Morgenthau's reading of prestige corresponds with our presentation of the material or 'associational' sources of status, below, but does not capture the second, social, element of our status framework that attends to the 'normative' sources of status. Hans J. Morgenthau, *Politics among Nations: The Struggle for Power and Peace*, 4th edn (New York: Alfred A. Knopf, 1967), pp. 70, 74.

10 Gilpin, Robert, *War and Change in World Politics* (New York: Cambridge University Press, 1981), pp. 30–33.

11 Daase, Christopher, Caroline Fehl, Anna Geis and Georgias Kalliarakis, eds, *Recognition in International Relations: Rethinking A Political Concept in A Global Context* (Basingstoke and New York: Palgrave Macmillan, 2015); Larson, Deborah Welch, T. V. Paul and William C. Wohlforth, 'Status and World Order', in Paul et al., *Status in World Politics*, pp. 13–17.

12 Krasner, Stephen D. *Structural Conflict: The Third World against Global Liberalism* (Berkeley: University of California Press, 1985); Morgenthau, *Politics among Nations*. See also Nayar and Paul, *India in the World Order*.

13 Perkovich, George, *India's Nuclear Bomb: The Impact on Global Proliferation* (New Delhi: Oxford University Press, 2002).

14 See, for instance, Nayar and Paul, *India in the World Order*, p. 4.

15 Volgy, Thomas J., Renato Corbetta, J. Patrick Rhamey Jr, Ryan G. Baird, and Keith A. Grant, 'Status Considerations in International Politics and the Rise of Regional Powers', in Paul et al., *Status in World Politics*, pp. 58–84.

16 There is a large literature on this subject, with 'neoclassical realist' writings prominent in recent years. See, for example, Lobell, Steven E., Norrin M. Ripsman and Jeffrey W. Taliaferro, eds, *Neoclassical Realism, the State, and Foreign Policy* (New York: Cambridge University Press, 2009).

17 Cooper, Andrew F., Richard A. Higgott, and Kim Richard Nossal, *Relocating Middle Powers: Australia and Canada in A Changing World Order* (Vancouver, BC: University of British Columbia Press, 1993).

18 de Carvalho, Benjamin and Jon Harald Sande Lie, 'Small States and Status Seeking: Norway's Quest for Higher Standing', in Benjamin de Carvalho and Iver B. Neumann, eds, *A Great Power Performance: Norway's Quest for Higher Standing* (Abingdon and New York: Routledge, 2015), pp. 56–72.

19 Paul et al., *Status in World Politics*; Larson, Deborah Welch and Alexei Shevchenko, 'Status Seekers: Chinese and Russian Responses to U.S. Primacy', *International Security*, vol. 34, no. 4 (2010), pp. 63–95.

20 Larson et al., 'Status and World Order', p. 7.

21 Ibid., pp. 8–9.

22 Deng, Yong, *China's Struggle for Status: the Realignment of International Relations* (New York: Cambridge University Press, 2008), see esp. pp. 22–38.

23 Evans, Gareth, 'Foreign Policy and Good International Citizenship', Address by the Minister for Foreign Affairs, Senator Gareth Evans, Canberra, 6 March 1990, www.gevans.org/speeches/old/1990/060390_fm_fpandgoodinter nationalcitizen.pdf (accessed on 26 November 2016). The authors are grateful to Nicholas Wheeler for drawing attention to this.

24 Carvalho and Lie, 'Small States and Status Seeking'.

25 Busby, Joshua W., 'Good States: Prestige and Reputational Concerns of Major Powers under Unipolarity', Paper presented at the Annual Meeting

of the American Political Science Association, Washington, DC, 1–4 December 2005.

26 Lebow, Richard Ned, 'Fear, Interest and Honour: Outlines of a Theory of International Relations', *International Affairs*, vol. 82, no. 3 (2006), pp. 431–448, p. 437.

27 Milner Jr, Murray, *Status and Sacredness: A General Theory of Status Relations and an Analysis of Indian Culture* (New York: Oxford University Press, 1994).

28 Ibid., p. 36.

29 Paul, T. V., ed., *Accommodating Rising Powers: Past, Present and Future* (New York: Cambridge University Press, 2016).

30 Brittingham, Michael Alan, 'China's Contested Rise: Sino–U.S. Relations and the Social Construction of Great Power Status', in Sujian Guo and Shiping Hua, eds, *New Dimensions of Chinese Foreign Policy* (Lanham MD and Plymouth: Lexington Books, 2007), pp. 83–108.

31 Nayar and Paul, *India in the World Order*, p. 10.

32 Basrur, 'India: A Major Power in the Making'.

33 Lebow, Richard Ned, *A Cultural Theory of International Relations* (Cambridge: Cambridge University Press, 2008).

34 Larson and Shevchenko, 'Status Seekers'.

35 Mukherjee, Rohan, 'Statuspolitik as Foreign Policy: Strategic Culture and India's Nuclear Behavior', Paper presented at the Workshop on 'The Impact of National Cultures on Foreign Policy Making in a Multipolar World', Berlin, 3–4 October 2014. Mukherjee's analysis draws partly on Sidhu, Waheguru Pal Singh, Pratap Bhanu Mehta and Bruce Jones, eds, *Shaping the Emerging World: India and the Multilateral Order* (Washington, DC: Brookings Institution Press, 2013).

36 Brennan, Geoffrey, and Philip Pettit, *The Economy of Esteem* (Oxford: Oxford University Press, 2004), p. 27.

37 Brennan and Pettit, *Economy of Esteem*, p. 13.

38 Keohane, Robert O., 'The Economy of Esteem and Climate Change', *St. Anthony's International Review*, vol. 5, no. 2 (2010), pp. 16–28, p. 19.

39 Keohane, 'The Economy of Esteem', p. 19.

40 Bourdieu, Pierre, 'The Forms of Capital', pp. 241–258 in John G. Richardson, ed., *Handbook of Theory and Research for the Sociology of Education* (New York: Greenwood Press, 1986), p. 243.

41 'About Social Capital', Kennedy School of Government, Harvard University, n.d., www.hks.harvard.edu/programs/saguaro/about-social-capital (accessed on 22 February 2015). See also Anthony, Denise L. and John L. Campbell, 'States, Social Capital and Cooperation: Looking Back on "Governing the Commons"', *International Journal of the Commons*, vol. 5, no. 2, (2011) pp. 284–302 (accessed on 22 February 2015).; Siisiäinen, Martti, 'Two Concepts of Social Capital: Bourdieu vs. Putnam', Paper presented at ISTR Fourth International Conference on 'The Third Sector: For What and for Whom?' Trinity College, Dublin, Ireland, 5–8 July 2000, http://c.ym cdn.com/sites/www.istr.org/resource/resmgr/working_papers_dublin/siisiainen. pdf (accessed on 22 February 2015).

42 de Lange, Deborah E., *Power and Influence: The Embeddedness of Nations* (New York: Palgrave Macmillan, 2010); Dominguez, Silvia and Celeste Watkins, 'Creating Networks for Survival and Mobility: Social Capital

Among African-American and Latin-American Low-income Mothers', *Social Problems*, vol. 50, no. 1 (2003), pp. 111–135; Kahler, Miles, *Networked Politics: Agency, Power and Governance* (Ithaca, NY: Cornell University Press, 2009); Wilson, Lou and Peter Mayer, 'Upward Mobility and Social Capital: Building Advantage through Volunteering', *Australian Policy Online*, 16 January 2007, http://apo.org.au/research/upward-mobility-and-social-cap ital-building-advantage-through-volunteering (accessed on 22 February 2015). For a more cautious view, see Maoz, Zeev,*Networks and Nations: The Evolution, Structure and Impact of International Networks, 1816–2001* (Cambridge: Cambridge University Press, 2011), esp. pp. 223–236.

43   Important examples include: Bajpai, Kanti, Saira Basit, and V. Krishnappa, eds, *India's Grand Strategy: History, Theory, Cases* (New Delhi/Abingdon: Routledge, 2014); Cohen, *India: Emerging Power*; Gordon, *India's Rise as an Asian Power*; Hall, Ian, ed., *The Engagement of India: Strategies and Responses* (Washington, DC: Georgetown University Press, 2014); Mohan, C. Raja, *Crossing the Rubicon: The Shaping of India's New Foreign Policy* (New York: Palgrave Macmillan, 2003); Malone, *Does the Elephant Dance?*; Pant, Harsh V., *Contemporary Debates in Indian Foreign and Security Policy* (Basingstoke: Palgrave Macmillan, 2012); Schaffer, Howard B. and Teresita C. Schaffer, *India at the Global High Table: The Quest for Regional Primacy and Strategic Autonomy* (Washington, DC: Brookings Institution Press, 2016); and Sullivan, Kate, ed., *Competing Visions of India in World Politics: India's Rise Beyond the West* (Basingstoke: Palgrave Macmillan, 2015).

44   Clunan, Anne L., 'Why Status Matters in World Politics', in Paul et al., *Status in World Politics*, pp. 273–296, p. 274.

45   Larson et al., 'Status and World Order', p. 13.

46   Larson et al., 'Status and World Order', p. 9.

47   Neumann, Iver B., 'Status is Cultural: Durkheimian Poles and Weberian Russians Seek Great Power Status', in Paul et al., *Status in World Politics*, pp. 85–112, p. 85.

48   As will become clear, our status-centred reading of 'the international' is primarily social, with the material underpinnings of status ordered through that society. Therefore, whether we speak of an international system or an international society, we implicitly refer to a contingent social order built on common – though certainly not universally accepted, and often contested – understandings and norms about what can be deemed status-enhancing. This is of course breaking substantially with an English School tradition that has been careful to distinguish between society and system, see, for example, Buzan, Barry, 'From International System to International Society: Structural Realism and Regime Theory Meet the English School', *International Organization*, vol. 47, no. 3 (1993), pp. 327–352.

49   Milner, *Status and Sacredness*, p. 36.

50   To underscore the social contingency of military power as the basis for status, Lebow notes that military power may cease to be status-enhancing, '[i]f there is a shift in the nature of standing, and especially one that delegitimizes the use of force for anything but the most immediate defensive purposes, or in humanitarian intervention with the backing of large segments of the world community', Lebow, 'Fear, Interest and Honour', pp. 431–448, p. 437.

51   Milner, *Status and Sacredness*, p. 35.

52 We thank Roy Allison for making the point that the contemporary global order is normatively plural. However, arguably, all normative orders are characterised by plurality in the sense of contestation and challenge, and we believe that a conception of dominant norms continues to be both representative of reality and analytically useful.

53 Milner, *Status and Sacredness*, p. 35.

54 Milner, *Status and Sacredness*, p. 36.

55 Schirm, Stefan A., 'Leaders In Need of Followers: Emerging Powers in Global Governance', *European Journal of International Relations*, vol. 16, no. 2 (June 2010), pp. 197–221.

56 Clunan, 'Why Status Matters in World Politics', p. 277.

57 See for example, Sullivan, *Is India a Responsible Nuclear Power?* where the conception of responsibility presented draws on Bukovansky, Mlada, Ian Clark, Robyn Eckersley, Richard Price, Christian Reus-Smit and Nicholas J. Wheeler, *Special Responsibilities: Global Problems and American Power* (Cambridge: Cambridge University Press, 2012).

58 Bull, Hedley, *The Anarchical Society: A Study of Order in World Politics*, 3rd edn (Basingstoke: Palgrave, 2002). For a contemporary theorising, see also: Loke, Beverley, 'Unpacking the Politics of Great Power Responsibility: Nationalist and Maoist China in International Order-building', *European Journal of International Relations*, vol. 22, no. 4 (December 2016), pp. 847–871.

59 Gerring, John, 'What Is a Case Study and What Is It Good For?' *American Political Science Review*, vol. 98, no. 2 (May, 2004), p. 342.

60 Burawoy, 'The Extended Case Method', in Michael Burawoy et al., *Ethnography Unbound: Power and Resistance in the Modern Metropolis* (Berkeley: University of California Press), pp. 271–287.

61 Burawoy, 'The Extended Case Method', p. 281.

62 Critics may cavil at our overlooking India's violation of the NPT norm against testing, but the 1998 tests did not bring any sign of the regime's collapse. Indeed, though Iran did point a finger at India when it was under pressure from the United States, the regime was strengthened by the restraints Teheran accepted under the eight-nation Joint Comprehensive Plan of Action agreed in July 2015.

63 'India Deserves UNSC Permanent Membership, Says PM Narendra Modi', *Economic Times* (8 June 2015), see: http://economictimes.indiatimes. com/articleshow/47578554.cms?utm_source=contentofinterest&utm_m edium=text&utm_campaign=cppst (accessed 22 July 2016).

64 For more on 'plausibility' as a test of a given historical narrative, see Reus-Smit, Christian, 'Reading History through Constructivist Eyes', *Millennium: Journal of International Studies*, vol. 37, no. 2 (2008), pp. 395–414.

65 Miller, Manjari Chatterjee, 'The Un-Argumentative Indian? Ideas about the Rise of India and Their Interaction with Domestic Structures', *India Review*, vol. 13, no. 1 (2014), pp. 1–14; Kate Sullivan, 'India's Ambivalent Projection of Self as a Global Power: Between Compliance and Resistance', in Sullivan, *Competing Visions of India in World Politics*, pp. 15–33.

2 Status without power in the Nehru era (1947–1964)

Introduction

This chapter explores India's attempts at seeking status during the period in which Jawaharlal Nehru led the country as prime minister and foreign minister, from Independence in 1947 until his death in 1964. Key to India's status seeking during this period was a weak focus on the *associational* sources of status. India's leadership resisted the build-up of material power, especially conventional military and nuclear power. India's economic power, too, remained largely a work in progress. The weak focus on associational sources of status also extended to the avoidance of alliance relationships with either of the dominant states of the time, the United States and the Soviet Union. Instead, India sought to carve out a strategic space distinct from the influence of these two antagonistic powers, adopting a commitment to non-alignment and, in 1961, joining and spearheading the Non-aligned Movement (NAM). Instead of integrating with the emerging US-led global capitalist economy, India adopted a defensive, post-colonial development model based on import substitution, high tariff barriers and self reliance.

Rather than seeking status through conformity with dominant norms, India's status-seeking efforts during this period exhibited innovation. Through the NAM and other institutions and processes, India engaged in 'counter-order' efforts that sought to effect a transformation of the two chief characteristics of the global system – the Cold War and the capitalist world economy – and to challenge the possession and testing of nuclear weapons. At the same time, India did conform to the norm of democratic statehood, a key marker of status in the eyes of the United States and its allies. However, while India's democratic institutions were stable, they remained vulnerable. Moreover, in another example of conformity, India's abjuration of nuclear weapons resonated with the emerging norms of non-proliferation backed by the dominant powers. Overall, these efforts had security-enhancing as well as status-enhancing aims. India's approach sought to build status without material power and aimed, in the long run, to utilise higher status to reconstruct the world for the achievement of greater security as well as other values.

India's early policies under the leadership of Jawaharlal Nehru, India's first prime minister and foreign minister after Independence, are not difficult to understand in the context of pre-independence thinking on international affairs within India. In the decades leading up to Independence, Nehru and other Indian nationalists – most associated with the Indian National Congress (INC), the premier nationalist organisation – arrived at a broad consensus on the kind of role India should play within international politics.[1] First, India could offer something qualitatively different to world affairs: rather than amassing hard power, a number of influential Indian nationalists saw an opportunity for India to challenge the prevailing psychology of fear and mistrust between nations through declarations of friendship and pacific intent. Such a role for India would, they believed, mitigate international tensions, serve as an example to other states, and bring 'morality' to the international realm. If successful, this recasting of the terms of inter-state relations would present a normative approach to the conduct of world politics, and, as chief innovator of that order, ultimately enhance India's global status. Second, along similar lines, India's avoidance of alignment with major powers and involvement in military alliances or pacts was certainly aimed at maintaining India's independence, but it, too, was a strategy aimed at lessening the fear and mistrust among states that heightened the potential for violence and war. Third, India's chances of fully overcoming its own direct experience of imperialism, would be heightened by seeking common cause with subject peoples across the globe, particularly in Africa and Asia. Each of these three elements contributed to a broad blueprint for India's independent foreign policy, and led to the predominantly 'counter-order' patterns of status seeking we go on to explore.

Overall, this period demonstrates a temporary rise in India's status. India's efforts at conflict mediation between the major powers and at rallying others around a particular Indian vision of a global counter order, particularly through the Afro-Asian group at the United Nations, the Bandung Conference in 1955 and the first non-aligned summit in 1961, led, in part, to higher status, though were in some ways also alienating to smaller states in the region. However, India's bitter defeat in the 1962 border war with China proved publicly that the Nehruvian brand of normative innovation was doomed to fail. Shunning material power, relying on declarations of friendship and pacific intent, and failing to establish security relationships with either of the major powers left India vulnerable. India's temporary status gains through its normative innovation were undermined by its weak levels of associational status, that is, through an absence of power. In sum, our account of this period problematises the realist understanding of material power as the central foundation for status by showing how India's early leaders purposefully de-prioritised military development, challenged material capability as a central criterion for status, sought to construct an alternative normative order in international politics that defied the logic of the Cold War, *and* gained a limited and temporary degree of status in doing so.

Dominant material associations and international norms in the Nehru era

In the introduction to this volume, we underscored the significance of *associations* with predominantly-valued objects and actors as sources of status as well as conformity with dominant *norms* in the international order.[2] In the early years of India's independent history, which international political associations were prevalent and which norms could be deemed dominant, and therefore status-enhancing, for a state such as India?

Associations with material power were significant in the post-1945 world order. The institutional design of the United Nations, established in 1945, reflected how the five permanent members of the Security Council collectively viewed themselves and each other as militarily and politically equipped to maintain international order and security.[3] Meanwhile, in the wake of the Second World War, from 1945, the United States and the USSR became locked in a military and ideological conflict that impacted many parts of the world, including Asia. As the Cold War progressed, the two superpowers grew in military and economic dominance, bolstered by extensive arsenals of nuclear weapons. By the 1960s, nuclear weapons had come to occupy front stage in the Cold War, especially in the crises over Berlin and Cuba. In 1950, the United States was in possession of 299 nuclear warheads in comparison to Russia's 5; between 1960 and 1964, the number of US warheads climbed from around 18,638 to 29,463, with Russia's arsenal expanding from 1627 to 5,242 warheads throughout the same period.[4] By 1964, the United Kingdom, France and China had also joined the ranks of the nuclear-armed powers.

Building on the material predominance of the United States and the USSR, the status of the superpowers also accrued from the way in which they socially constructed their shared rivalry. As Buzan has argued, the idea of a global order structured through bipolarity 'unquestionably served the interests of the two superpowers' by positioning them and their ideological conflict at the heart of world politics: it 'helped to justify their assertions of hegemony and/or suzerainty over their respective camps ... it enabled them to form a kind of diplomatic club from which all others could be excluded'.[5] As a result, many, if not all, states in the international system faced a choice between an association with one of the two superpowers, or no association at all, with each path offering distinctive material and social advantages and disadvantages.

The world wars and the Cold War firmly placed material power at the centre of interstate politics. US strategy became premised on the 'assumption that the Soviet Union intended to engineer a global expansion of the Communist system'[6] and applied American material power to the containment of communism in Asia, seeking to retain global space for capitalist expansion.[7] In Asia, therefore, bandwagoning with the United States stood as a key source of associational status in the early decades of the Cold War. For many Asian states, including India, joining the anti-communist cause was crucial to securing acceptance and status from the perspective of the United States. At the same time, while the expansion of the USSR was comparatively less comprehensive, centring primarily (and intensively) on neighbouring areas, its size and geographical reach meant that Soviet influence would also become significant in Asia, particularly in North Korea, and later North Vietnam and Afghanistan.

In terms of the *normative sources of status*, the ideological confrontation between capitalism and communism, mirroring the military rivalry between the United States and the USSR, respectively, was a major structuring feature of international order during the Cold War. While the two rivals differed vastly in their preferred forms of political governance and economic development, they frequently collaborated in the establishment and (frequently inharmonious) dominance of system-regulating institutions, such as the United Nations, and stability-enhancing moves such as efforts to limit nuclear proliferation.

Economically, the United States enjoyed an 'unchallenged position' after the Second World War, including 'technological leadership across all sectors, dominance of world output and unrivalled economic competitive position on the world market, the international role of the dollar as the only effective currency and the dominant place of US foreign direct investment'.[8] Underpinning and legitimising this economic dominance was a liberal doctrine that incorporated a staunch commitment to capitalist enterprise, small government, and openness to foreign investment and trade.[9] Hence, India's efforts to achieve economic development along democratic lines assumed special, international significance.[10]

Overall, despite the Soviet challenge, throughout the Cold War the United States stood as the predominant power in a Western-dominated international system,[11] and, on account of its superior resources it would often be viewed from New Delhi as a needed partner – both in terms of military and economic aid.[12] In the opening decades of the Cold War, therefore, the acquisition of material power and alignment with one of the superpowers, where the United States stood most influential, can be deemed crucial sources of associational status. India, as we shall show, did not develop either of these key associations. In terms of international norms, liberal democracy and capitalism stood dominant, though challenged by communism. India embraced liberal democracy, but did not accept or practise the established forms of capitalist or communist economics.

Associational status seeking in the Nehru era

Material attributes

Economic power

Jawaharlal Nehru's early vision of Indian power centred on the need to consolidate and strengthen a materially strong nation as a means of avoiding future conquest and foreign rule.[13] Achieving material parity with the nations of the developed world was the only means of securing India's freedom in the long term, and India's development of an industrial base and investment in science and technology were the major steps taken towards this goal.[14]

In his search to unify, modernise and strengthen the Indian state, Nehru's primary commitment was to economic development.[15] British rule had shaped India's economy according to imperial interests and for many nationalists the Indian freedom struggle had become synonymous with ending the drain of wealth from the sub-continent.[16] Accelerated economic growth was one means of negating the devastating effects of colonialism on India's overall wealth, and addressing the pressing issues of basic literacy, housing and welfare. This led to the decision to adopt a mixed economy and work towards a model of economic autarky based on import substitution, heavy industrialisation and the build-up of infrastructures such as dams, electricity and transportation.[17] India's foreign trade as a percentage of its GDP remained a low 9 per cent in the last year of his leadership.[18] India under Nehru aimed for the alleviation of poverty, but also for Indian self-sufficiency, an aspiration that did not materialise in his lifetime, or for that matter after him.

On average, the Indian economy grew, in real terms, at 3.5 to 4 per cent each year in the 1950s and then slowed to around 2.5 per cent from 1961 to 1966 owing to drought conditions that caused a significant decline in agricultural production.[19] In the 1950s and 1960s, India ran increasing trade deficits and struggled with food shortages that necessitated urgent recourse to outside assistance.[20] As a result, India became substantially dependent on both bilateral and multilateral foreign aid. Despite clear limitations to India's capacity to bargain in the international realm, however, Nehru believed India's autonomy, in the form of non-alignment, could not be compromised. In an early speech to the US Congress in October 1949, he emphasised the need for India to alleviate poverty through 'greater production, more equitable distribution, better education and better health' and emphasised that 'though our economic potential is great, its conversion into finished wealth will need much mechanical and technological aid'.[21] However, Nehru also underscored that 'we do not seek any material advantage in exchange for any part of our hard-won freedom'.[22]

Indeed, broadly speaking, India did succeed in maintaining economic independence. In the 1960s, India emerged as the 'economic aid priority' of the United States, as part of the broader US political strategy to contain communism in Asia and enhance the space for private enterprise.[23] However, even while over several years US administrations attempted to link food assistance to adjustments in foreign and domestic policy, the Indian leadership remained firm in refusing aid with conditions attached.[24]

Military power

Nehru's post-Independence focus was on 'building state power, but not state military power': from 1947 to 1964, India made only limited investments in defence.[25] A 1948 report by British scientist P. M. S. Blackett, commissioned by the Indian government, made recommendations to maintain India's defence spending at 2 per cent of GDP.[26] India's military expenditure hovered at this level throughout the 1950s,[27] and in dollar terms stood at roughly a quarter of China's military spending in both 1950 and 1960.[28]

There are a number of reasons for India's lesser focus on military power in the early years. In part, India's military modesty stemmed from the overall limitations of the Indian economy, which led to a lower prioritisation of military armament in relation to more pressing developmental needs such as industrialisation.[29]

Many Indian nationalists also viewed India's armed forces as a financial drain, and understood military power primarily as a tool of oppression.[30] But at a broader level, in the decades before independence the nationalist Indian outlook on world affairs had become dominated by 'a sense of alienation from the course of European politics'.[31] Nehru and mainstream nationalists rejected what they saw as the materialism of the West, which they believed had driven European countries to pursue colonial conquest in order to satisfy the material appetites of their citizens.[32] The imperialist tendencies of these states were the major cause of conflict and tension in Europe. War, many nationalists claimed (with the notable exception of Subhas Chandra Bose), was not prevented by the build-up of arms and the formation of military alliances and pacts but in fact stemmed from the fears and suspicions *caused* by arms build-ups and alliances.[33]

Thus, Indian nationalists largely (though not exclusively) agreed that the appropriate policy for India was to declare peace and friendship towards its neighbours. Peace would come only when states no longer sought to exploit one another; that is, world peace depended on an end to imperialism. What a number of nationalists were effectively proposing, was a non-exploitative role for India in world affairs that in turn would earn status, and as a result, security. Rajendra Prasad, for example, a key figure in the INC and the first president of India, declared in 1934,

> India having no designs on others will not then need a large army either for its protection against foreigners or for internal peace which will stand guaranteed by the goodwill of other inhabitants. Having no designs on others she will be able to claim immunity from the evil designs of others and her safety will be buttressed and protected by the goodwill of the world at large.[34]

Significant to our account of India's status seeking is the belief among many Indian nationalists that a proactive leadership role for India would contribute significantly to world peace.[35] Non-alignment should be seen in this context. India was particularly well placed to lead a much-needed peaceful revolution in world politics, it was argued, owing to the perceived positive record of the expediency and rectitude of non-violent political methods during India's independence movement, under the leadership of Mohandas Karamchand Gandhi. Discussions within the Constituent Assembly Debates in 1948 over Article 51 of the Indian Constitution, for example, revealed a widespread affirmation of the unique moral role India must play internationally.[36]

Domestically, alternatives to abstention from the acquisition of material capability certainly were expressed during the early years after independence, though not as part of the mainstream political discourse. K. M. Panikkar, an academic and one of Nehru's most respected diplomats, and G. S. Bajpai, whom Nehru had selected as secretary-general for external affairs in 1948, both argued in favour of India's acquisition of strong defence capabilities.[37] Bajpai for example, saw 'danger … in the unqualified condemnation of "power politics"' and argued that material power would enable India to fulfil her 'supreme aim' of peace, since its use would be curbed by 'India's determination to use power only when forced to defend her freedom, her sense of values and her way of life'.[38]

While ideas based upon the necessity of hard power to back up India's moral message were in circulation, they did not gain mainstream currency until after India's defeat in the 1962 border war with China. Nehru's approach to China, as another ancient and enduring civilisation in Asia, had been one of friendly interest and a desire to work in partnership towards a pan-Asian identity and a peaceful world order. He made a priority of Indo-Chinese friendship and believed that 'the future of Asia and to some extent the world depends on this'.[39] The blueprint for peaceful coexistence that emerged in 1954 as a treaty between the two countries, *panchsheel*,[40] promised an area of peace in Asia that Nehru hoped might one day extend beyond the region. China's Tibet policy was a cause of concern and suspicion for some, and by the late 1950s, Home Minister Sardar Vallabhbhai Patel, G. S. Bajpai and even the Indian president, Rajendra Prasad, were vigorously warning of a Chinese threat. But Nehru remained convinced that mutual understanding with China was an adequate means of meeting India's security needs. His dominance of India's foreign policy, his unquestioned authority as India's leader at home and in the world, and his strategy of rewarding those who shared his views, meant that few were seriously equipped to challenge him.

The result was that India was ill-prepared for the war against China in 1962.[41] The shock of the war and India's defeat overturned much of what Nehru had built up and believed in. It eroded his personal standing both at home and abroad. It was widely felt as a national humiliation and the collapse of India's international status. Even Indians who were sympathetic to Nehru conceded that India had 'failed to develop a realistic view of its defense needs' and suggested that reconciling the Gandhian philosophy of nonviolence in relations with other countries was impossible in 'a world which had not disavowed war and the use of force in general'.[42] The official view, published in the 1966 report of the Committee on the Indian Foreign Service, the first and only ever audit of India's foreign policy bureaucracy, was that the experience with China had 'wrought a profound change in our thinking by destroying the illusion that unilateral demonstration of peace and goodwill can be a substitute for strength and ability to defend ourselves'.[43]

Thus, the 1962 war with China laid the foundation for India's gradual expansion of its military power. India's energised defence strategy was targeted at meeting a threat from Chinese forces along its northern border, and later from Chinese-backed Pakistani aggression. But it was also aimed at rebuilding India's international status and avoiding a repeat humiliation.

Nuclear power

In keeping with a rejection of the acquisition of military power, India under Nehru also rejected nuclear weapons. But Nehru's perceptions were mixed. He thought nuclear weapons to be immoral and sought their abolition, yet was not ready to issue a firm unilateral commitment to this end. In contrast, his defence minister, V. K. Krishna Menon, was adamant in his rejection of nuclear weapons.[44] Nehru worried that 'one accident, one irrational decision, or one wrong move might very well spell an end for everything living', but acknowledged that deterrence prevented war between the United States and the Soviet Union.[45] Thus, even as he advocated universal nuclear disarmament, Nehru kept the door to nuclear weapons just a little open. Shortly before his death in 1964, on a memorandum written by the pro-bomb nuclear scientist, Homi Bhabha, Nehru wrote that nuclear technology offered the 'built-in advantage' of defence use should the need arise.[46] Nevertheless, the fact remains that even the 1962 catastrophe did not alter his policy of abjuring nuclear weapons.

Nehru's preoccupation was with the developmental promise of atomic energy rather than its military potential. In April 1948, the Constituent Assembly debated an Atomic Energy Bill, which provided for 'the development and control of atomic energy and for purposes connected therewith'.[47] For Nehru, atomic energy could play an important role in the economic development of the nation, providing an additional power source for India's industrialisation, and potentially proving itself to have many profitable applications in other domains such as agriculture and medicine. Introducing the Bill, Nehru clarified, it is not from the point of view of war that I am placing this Bill before this House but rather from the point of view of the future progress of India and the Indian people and the world at large. If we do not set about it now, taking advantage of the processes that go towards the making of atomic energy, and join in the band of scholars and researchers who are trying to develop it, we will be left behind and we shall possibly only just have the chance to follow in the trail of others. That is not good enough for any country, least of all a country with the vast potential and strength that India possesses.[48]

The voices in the Assembly that responded to Nehru's initial statement were predominantly in support of the Bill, and spoke strongly in favour an outright rejection of the destructive uses of nuclear technology. Nehru's only reference to the military uses of nuclear technology in the debate was couched firmly in terms of defence:

Of course, if we are compelled as a nation to use it for other purposes, possibly no pious sentiments of any of us will stop the nation from using it that way. But I do hope that our outlook in regard to this atomic energy is going to be a peaceful one for the development of human life and happiness and not one of war and hatred.[49]

The Bill was passed, and so the Indian state took the decision to embrace atomic energy, opening the door to India's eventual nuclear weapons development. Yet much of the debate centred on how the pursuit of an atomic energy programme presented an opportunity for India to make an ethical contribution to a new human era, the atomic era. This again positioned India in a moral leadership role. A non-violent approach to international affairs, symbolised by a rejection of power and a rejection of the atom bomb, was based on an ideology that envisioned a post-imperial age, and a future inspired by forces for peace rather than struggles for monopolies over material goods. India's moral stewardship of atomic development, it was envisioned, would bring the requisite status to drive the development of a new moral global order. Almost a decade later, this commitment appeared to abide. Nehru, at the inauguration of India's first nuclear reactor 'Aspara' at Trombay in January 1957, claimed:

No man can prophesy the future. But I should like to say on behalf of my Government – and I think I can say with some assurance on behalf of any future Government of India – that whatever might happen, whatever the circumstances, we shall never use this atomic energy for evil purposes.[50]

Relations with the dominant powers

From Independence onwards, India sought – not always successfully – to resist proximity to the two Cold War rivals and their camps. It did so by avoiding participation or membership in military alliances and pacts, and by refraining from accepting forms of external assistance, whether military or economic, that bore conditions. This approach was forged in the decades preceding Independence, when, broadly speaking, Indian nationalists held mixed views towards both the Soviet Union and the United States. As T. A. Keenleyside notes:

> Indians admired the domestic social and economic progress in the Soviet Union, but were worried by the doctrinaire Soviet attitude to ideology, by indications of repression and violence and by signs during the war of an inchoate imperialist policy. With respect to the United States, they were once again impressed by domestic economic developments, by the emphasis on social equality and individual liberty and by the presence of democratic institutions, but sceptical of the dogmatic American commitment to free enterprise and capitalism, and indications of a neo-imperialist outlook.[51]

Ambivalence towards the two superpowers led to a policy that would allow India to preserve its distance from the dominant powers. The ultimate decision was to adopt a policy of non-alignment. Nehru, in the first public statement[52] of his government's intentions for India in the international realm, declared in 1946 that India was to engage with the world,

> as a free nation with our own policy and not merely as a satellite of another nation. We hope to develop close and direct contacts with other nations and to co-operate with them in the furtherance of world peace and freedom. We propose, as far as possible, to keep away from the power politics of groups, aligned against one another, which have led in the past to world wars and which may again lead to disasters on an even vaster scale.[53]

Non-alignment, as the policy came to be called, was not simply a policy of strategic autonomy. An extension of the Indian critique of the build-up of military power, it stood as a normative framework that critiqued prevailing patterns of aggression and injustice in world politics. In practical terms, it was a response to the realities of a tense international situation and India's urgent domestic developmental needs. Peace was essential for the freedom, consolidation and development of impoverished nations across the world. It was therefore imperative to shield a still fragmented and weak India from any enmeshment in conflict. Moreover, by refusing to take sides, India's non-aligned stance could provide avenues for a potentially status-enhancing mediating role in world affairs. In April 1948, in response to mounting Cold War tensions, Nehru declared in a letter to India's chief ministers,

> I am convinced that India's role should be as far as possible to continue to remain apart from any particular bloc. This is safest for India and it may in the future give some chance to India to play a pacific role. We cannot place this too high as we are not strong enough at present to exercise much influence. Nevertheless it would be equally wrong to ignore the fact that we can and do count in international affairs. It would be a very short-sighted policy for us to line up with any group in order to gain some temporary advantage.[54]

Non-alignment thus aimed both at maintaining India's freedom of action, and offered the possibility of a practical – and status-enhancing – role for India as global peacemaker. These aims saw mixed success. India was able to play a conspicuous mediating role in the Korean War in 1952, at the 1954 Geneva Conference on Indo-China, and in the Suez Crisis of 1956, and began contributing substantially to UN peacekeeping forces. These activities greatly enhanced India's international status.[55] However, India was far less successful at maintaining a non-aligned and independent stance in matters relating to its own national security.

When the Indo–Pakistan dispute over Kashmir was brought before the Security Council in 1948, Indian foreign policy elites met with surprise what they perceived as the 'active partisanship for Pakistan' among the great powers.[56] For Nehru, the Kashmir question was 'not being discussed fairly' and India was being faced with 'considerable pressure'.[57] The perceived partiality of the UN Security Council led Nehru to note that 'the achievement of independence and a desire to maintain our own foreign relations, free of attachment to blocs, has brought us sharply against the ugly forces of power politics'.[58] Apart from negatively affecting India's reputation and stature, the potential for external interference on the issue of Kashmir presented a tangible threat to India's national integrity. This negative experience of the Security Council opened Indian eyes to the realities of superpower politics within the United Nations, a wariness of their designs on newly emerging post-colonial societies, and a keen sense of Indian vulnerabilities.[59] From the late 1940s onwards, India sought continually to keep the Kashmir issue away from the Council. From 1955 an implicit alignment with the USSR emerged as India grew to rely on the Soviet veto in the Security Council to block unacceptable resolutions on the Kashmir question.[60] Indo–Soviet relations had borne little fruit from 1947 to 1954, owing to Stalin's 'view of post-colonial governments as tools of Western imperialism' and opposition to India's policy of non-alignment.[61] In the post-Stalinist period, however, the USSR shifted from its neutral stance on the Kashmir dispute owing to both a change in leadership, and Pakistan's joining of the Southeast Asia Treaty Organization (SEATO)[62] in 1954 and the Central Treaty Organization (CENTO) in 1955.[63] In effect, Nehru's India came to rely on the Soviet Union in what was clearly a deviation from his determination to keep the great powers at arm's length.

The most seismic challenge to India's policy of non-alignment, however, came with the 1962 Sino–Indian war. India's defeat in the war necessitated outside military assistance, and from 1962, India accepted military aid from both the United States and the Soviet Union.[64] The thirty-day war in October–November 1962 impelled India to seek out modern weaponry equal to the task of responding to forces of the People's Republic of China (PRC) on the northeastern border.[65] Nehru accepted large-scale military assistance from the United States during the conflict. Faced with 'the extraordinary sweep and speed' of PRC forces advancing in a second assault, Nehru allegedly even went so far as to request urgent and massive US air intervention to protect North Indian cities and attack Chinese lines of communications.[66] This request was allegedly met favourably by the US government but was not fulfilled owing to China's sudden unilateral declaration of a ceasefire and strategic retreat.[67] However, India went on to request $500 million of military assistance from the United States, to be spread over five years, ultimately receiving $120 million.[68] US reluctance to commit more generously to long-term defence arrangements with India stemmed from its long-term provision of military and other aid to Pakistan and concerns about the continued tensions between the two South Asian neighbours.[69] Potential progress in late 1963 on a more expansive agreement with the United States in support of Indian defence modernisation collapsed with the assassination of President Kennedy and, in May 1964, the death of Nehru.[70] As Chari observes, 'the only major arms producing nation towards whom India could have turned was the Soviet Union'.[71] From 1964 onwards India sourced the bulk of its tanks, naval vessels, combat aircraft, and other defence equipment, including helicopters and light arms, from the Soviet Union.[72]

The 1962 war thus necessitated alignments in both directions, and certainly forced India to break with its policy of resisting proximity to the major powers. As Michael Brecher described it, 'the foreign policy of Nehru's India began to change ... from "equidistance," in relation to the superpowers, to "equal proximity" to Moscow and Washington'.[73] Non-alignment was succeeded by 'bi-alignment',[74] and was left severely damaged, if not completely shattered, as a security policy.

Over all, during the Nehru era, associations with predominantly-valued objects and actors were not simply deprioritised, but were, at least until 1962, actively avoided. While, it is clear that the limited economic possibilities of the Indian state were a factor in the reluctance to engage in high defence spending and military acquisition, when it came to alliances and the question of nuclear weapons, ideas appeared far more important. Indian ideas about associational status were radically different from the prevailing norms, and indeed sought to challenge them.

Normative status seeking in the Nehru era

Responses to dominant global norms

In the introduction to this volume, we drew on the existing literature on status to underscore that the 'highest levels of status are sometimes associated with innovation'.[75] In other words, status-seeking states may seek status not through conformity with established, accepted norms, but by seeking to project alternative criteria. Perhaps the most ambitious version of such a strategy is to seek to create an alternative system of norms – a 'counter'-status order.

In relation to the associational sources of status, as we have seen above, India rejected military build-up and the development of nuclear weapons, and resisted, as far as possible, associations with the dominant powers. Instead, India under Nehru effectively sought a reconfiguration of the very sources of international status altogether. Non-alignment, in particular, was more than a strategy of distance from major powers: as a philosophy it challenged the traditional way in which world politics had been conducted. It manifested in attempts to assist in the decolonisation efforts of other emerging nations; to negate through disarmament the concentration of power that permitted imperialism and war; to mediate, where possible, between warring parties; to dismantle imperial power structures by strengthening the United Nations; and to encourage a more equitable distribution of resources between nations and peoples.

The audience for such an endeavour was therefore global – India sought status from both major powers and a broad constituency of newly decolonised or decolonising, as well as other developing countries. India attempted – and occasionally succeeded – to mediate between the central conflicting parties in a tension-filled Cold War context. Its leaders sought common cause with subject peoples everywhere, especially in Asia and Africa. For a time, this strategy met with success. However, a status-seeking strategy based on high-minded moral leadership was vulnerable to accusations of hypocrisy: India's own use of force in Goa and elsewhere and its reliance on American military assistance in 1962 came under enormous international scrutiny. India's attempts at status seeking through the projection of its vision of a counter order also suffered at times from a disconnect between India's self-perceived stature in the international realm and the perceptions of others. Unluckily, just as Nehru was beginning to publicly preach India's commitment to – and special credentials in – the fostering of world peace, the partition of the Subcontinent unfolded, unleashing inconceivable violence.

Nehru was extremely conscious that the eyes of the world were watching developments in India and Pakistan. He saw the upholding of principles in both the domestic realm – particularly on the issue of the integration of the princely states, which in the case of Hyderabad eventually involved the use of force – and in conduct with other countries as critical to India's international standing. When the Indo–Pakistani dispute over the political status of Jammu and Kashmir erupted in 1947, Nehru was determined to pursue peaceful channels for its resolution, both to spare India the consequences of investing in war, but equally as a moral statement and a means of upholding India's reputation in the eyes of the world. In January 1948, India referred the Kashmir dispute to the Security Council of the United Nations, with – to India – dissatisfying results. Nehru's justification for doing so was that 'we wanted to avoid, in so far as this was possible, any development which would lead to war'.[76] Ultimately, India's attempt to lead in the establishment of a counter order was vulnerable on account of its material weakness, whose cost was the defeat by China in 1962.

Nonetheless, a head-start as a sizable post-colonial state after a dramatic freedom struggle and an insistence upon independent policies from the dominant powers pointed to an obvious place for India as a prime mover of a counter-order movement. From the 1920s onwards, a growing consensus emerged within the Indian National Congress that

India's freedom struggle could and must have a broader international impact.[77] The Conference of Oppressed Nationalities held in Brussels in February 1927 provided an unprecedented forum for direct contact between Afro-Asian leaders and proved a formative experience in the development of Nehru's international outlook.[78] Indian interest in engagement with other new and emerging states thus grew from the shared experience of colonial domination, but it was also accompanied by a realisation that these states faced similar challenges in the form of political consolidation, military weakness, economic development, social progress and the provision of basic services. Such overlapping preoccupations provided a foundation for a first forum for Asian cooperation, the Asian Relations Conference (ARC), convened in New Delhi in March 1947, some months before Indian independence. The ARC brought together representatives of various Asian countries for the exchange of views on common problems such as movements for freedom, migration, racial and cultural problems and the challenges of economic development and social services.[79] The discussion unavoidably touched upon national interests and sensitivities, too. Nehru took care in his inaugural speech to underline that 'in this conference there are no leaders and no followers [since] all countries of Asia have to meet together on an equal basis in a common task and endeavour'.[80] However, fears of Indian or Chinese domination did find their expression in the conference: a Burmese delegate suggested that while Western domination had been a terrible experience, to be ruled by an Asian power would be far worse.[81] Ceylon and Malaysia expressed similar sentiments. Such attitudes, together with what some described as a display of Indo–Chinese rivalry at the conference, hinted at the challenges that would face India's future multilateral efforts. At the ARC, however, these portents were subsumed by a more positive set of discussions.[82] Most delegates left the conference sharing a sense of the historic nature of the meeting, together with a deeper awareness of Asian neighbours and their concerns and the political and economic challenges that lay ahead for countries in the region.[83]

Nehru was keen to stress that India's approach to other Asian countries was to foster cooperation rather than to lead, and during a session of the United Nations Commission for Asia and the Far East in 1948 had emphasised that 'this business of any country thinking of itself as the leader of others smacks too much of a superiority complex which is not desirable in organisations working together for the common good'.[84] However, within Nehru's approach and attitude to cooperating with other countries was a deep ambivalence, since he could not help but see a key role for India. Indeed, a special responsibility is cast on India. India realises it and other countries realise it also. The responsibility is not necessarily for leadership, but for taking the initiative sometimes and helping others to cooperate.[85]

In the 1940s, 1950s and 1960s, the Indian counter-order effort took the form of advocacy for developing countries and fostering Afro–Asian cooperation in a way that would eventually, and indirectly, lead to the emergence of the Non-Aligned Movement. As a great believer in the United Nations, Nehru wished to strengthen it through India's active participation. He initially viewed the UN as a platform, free from entanglements with either of the two Cold War blocs, that would become the great enabler of international cooperation.[86] Indian involvement in the Afro–Asian Group was central to these efforts. During debates over the Korean War, an Arab–Asian Group emerged that provided safety in numbers in casting votes of abstention in the face of multiple US resolutions, and thus a degree of resistance to the pressure of Western countries.[87] Moreover, the Korean War provided an unparalleled opportunity for India to be involved in high-profile mediation between the East and the West. This cemented a belief among the Arab–Asian Group that Third World countries had a vital stake in the East–West confrontation and that they should, and could, play a role in promoting peace.[88] From this initial cooperation of Asian and Arab members emerged the Afro–Asian Group, and over time its views gained recognition as a recurring feature in the General Assembly, in similar measure to the existing Latin American caucus or group of Atlantic Pact countries. The Group was centred upon no clear ideology and was in that sense non-aligned. As a collective, it grew able to derive a shielding and protecting function from the United Nations which defended the security and interests of smaller and weaker powers.[89]

Rajeshwar Dayal, India's permanent representative to the UN in the first half of the 1950s, recalls how India was 'by far the largest and most influential member of the Group' and 'came to be regarded in the popular perception as the leader'.[90] Yet, reflecting the broader Indian position, Dayal eventually became frustrated with the Group. He recalled that, 'In the course of time I had begun to feel that India was too big and consequential an international power to be confined to the somewhat limited context of the Group, which concerned itself with race and anticolonialism rather than wider global political issues'.[91] An Indian concern with both championing and rising above the affairs and interests of smaller, weaker countries and taking a stand on issues of greater global consequence emerged as a repeating pattern. It reflected a quest for international status that was global in orientation, and could not be entirely satisfied only through a developing-country following. As a result, India frequently found itself stranded in an in-between space, unable or unwilling to interact on equal terms with major global players while appearing competitive or domineering from the perspective of other developing states.

India's at times alienating approach to projecting its counter-order norms became evident at the first Afro–Asian Conference at Bandung in 1955, too. While some viewed Bandung as 'Nehru's most significant contribution to the establishment of a new World Order', others noted how 'Nehru came to the Bandung Conference as the leader of Asia but left it as an outsider'.[92] Much of the groundwork that served as an enabler of the 'Bandung Spirit' had come from a decade of Nehru's consistent championing of the 'Asian viewpoint' in global forums.[93] As such, the conference in some sense marked the distillation of those efforts and the apex of India's Asian leadership.[94]

But four elements of Indian participation at Bandung proved damaging to India's reputation in the eyes of other participants. One complication prior to the conference was the success of India's behind-the-scenes role at the Geneva Conference in 1954, which met to discuss the restoration of peace in Indo-China. India had not been invited, but had enjoyed unexpected success through corridor diplomacy. Apart from both India and Nehru's international standing at the time, India's success at Geneva also derived from the collective stand that had been taken on the Indo-China issue by the Colombo Powers – Burma, Ceylon, India, Indonesia and Pakistan – earlier that year.[95] When India was invited to chair the supervisory commission set up to implement the terms of the Geneva Agreement, this was greatly to the annoyance of the Colombo powers, especially Ceylon and Indonesia.[96] A second irritant to India emerged from Nehru's prior insistence on inviting the People's Republic of China to appear for the first time in an international conference. Nehru's attempt to cultivate China on 'a stage set … with conscious deliberation' seemed to backfire.[97] For one thing, he committed the diplomatic *faux pas* of introducing the Chinese premier, Zhou Enlai, to the other delegates, a gesture the latter allegedly found highly patronising.[98] For another, Bandung delivered Zhou Enlai a successful personal debut on the international stage at the precise moment that Nehru's own stature was diminishing. With his 'courtesy, moderation and reasonableness', the Chinese premier earned for himself the nickname 'the Bandung Gentleman'.[99] The third damaging Indian contribution consisted of Nehru's impatient pronouncements on the 'meaning and virtues of non-alignment', which alienated many of the conference participants. While already highly critical of the membership of some participants in Western military alliances, Nehru had expounded 'with some impatience' on the virtues of non-alignment for the countries of Asia and Africa and condemned the decision of certain countries to join military pacts since they brought insecurity rather than security.[100]

The general response had not been positive. Pakistan denounced the suggestion that national decisions were to be justified to India or anyone else.[101] Other West-leaning delegates also expressed displeasure at Nehru's statements. Smaller countries such as the Philippines and Thailand felt that they needed such alliances in a way that India did not. From this perspective, Nehru's denunciation of any kind of military alliance was therefore particularly insensitive.[102] The Philippine foreign minister, Carlos Romulo, would later describe how Nehru had 'alienated the goodwill of many delegates' through his 'pronounced propensity to be dogmatic, impatient, irascible, and unyielding, especially in the face of opposition'.[103]

Finally, goodwill towards India was dented yet further by Nehru's role – for reasons that were unclear at the time – in blocking the Indonesian attempt to establish a permanent Asian–African conference secretariat.[104] Such an agency would have facilitated a more colla- borative approach to Asian–African cooperation and maintained a prominent position for Indonesia within subsequent Asian–African activities.[105] Nehru's reluctance was interpreted as an attempt by India to retain a monopoly over Asian affairs.[106]

While the Bandung Conference did little to benefit India's reputation in the eyes of other participants, its success could, however, be seen in the conference's final achievement of a unanimous communiqué, demon- strating a measure of Afro–Asian solidarity, even in the face of what emerged initially as a broad spectrum of irreconcilable sentiments and opinions. Nehru's outline of the basic tenets of Indian non-alignment was included in the ten-point 'declaration on promotion of world peace and cooperation'. Moreover, within the United Nations an informal community sharing an interest in the eradication of colonialism and racial discrimination emerged as an institutional locus for the mapping of the Bandung spirit. Dayal recounts how after 1955 the Afro–Asian Group became a 'force to be reckoned with', expanding to comprise more than half of all UN members and emerge as the most powerful of its regional groupings.[107] Nonetheless, one Bandung historian suggests that 'the quieter alienation of Southeast Asian leaders from any form of Indian leadership was truly long-term'.[108]

Efforts to stage new conferences were at work elsewhere during this period. In 1956, the same year in which Nehru rejected Sukarno's suggestion to convene a second Bandung, a meeting took place in Brioni, Yugoslavia in July, between Nehru, President Nasser of Egypt and President Tito of Yugoslavia. While the tripartite meeting had no formal outcome, it cemented close ties between the three men which would see them working in consultation on major global problems.[109] Their shared desire to maintain a distance from Cold War alliances provided for similarities of approach on foreign policy issues that transcended their divergent political systems and continental contexts. Their unity of outlook boded well for a heterogeneous movement of states united by a common critique of the prevailing international order.

Somewhat surprisingly, however, the emergence of what would become formally known as the Non-Aligned Movement revealed an increased Indian wariness of collective groupings. While the first in a series of summit conferences that began in Belgrade in September of 1961 was sponsored by Egypt and Yugoslavia with the support of India, Indonesia, Ghana and Mali, Nehru had initially been wary of the gathering, which he anticipated would simply provide another anti-colonial forum in an era when, to his mind, classical colonialism was no longer a dominant force in world affairs.[110] Nonetheless, once Nasser and Tito had decided to proceed with or without his support, he requested India's name be added to the list of original sponsors. At the Belgrade summit, Nehru sidestepped debates on colonialism and insisted on discussing broader global issues. In the context of heightened Cold War tensions, he believed that the danger of nuclear war was the most pressing concern and demanded urgent attention from the assembly of the Non-Aligned.[111] This approach earned him little favour among the other conference delegates. While the Western press commented on India's 'pre-eminence among the Belgrade participants' and Nehru's 'prestige and influence among the uncommitted world', he faced 'violent' criticism from other summit members who were disappointed at the apparent decline in his revolutionary, anti-colonial stance.[112] Yet as the conference progressed, Nehru found some success in his attempt to shift the priorities of the summit, steering it 'out of the old ruts of ritual opposition to colonialism, imperialism and racism' and securing a prominent place in the summit communiqué for the problem of peace in a nuclear world.[113] Nehru's biographer, Sarvepalli Gopal, described the Belgrade conference as the leader's 'last triumph in world affairs'.[114] However, support for his approach had been thin on the ground at the meeting itself, and as China mounted a campaign of anti-Indian pro-paganda from outside the bounds of the conference, the cost of attempting to agenda-set beyond the immediate interests of the parti-cipants was an increasingly ambivalent attitude towards India on the part of many African and Asian states. India's comparative size, resources, and global ambitions, plus its maturity as a state well over a decade into its independence, had again rendered it an uncomfortable outsider at Belgrade.

As these examples make clear, early Indian attempts to seek status and project a particularly Indian counter order were not straightforward. A reluctance to engage in groupings that pursued a narrower focus, and a domination of the procedure and output of any meeting once India became involved, revealed that Nehru was prepared to engage in only a certain kind of international collaboration, one that took a global focus and placed no limitations on India's international conduct. An Indian reluctance to form any kind of formal alliance or institutionalised organisation emerged, since these kinds of grouping were susceptible to manipulation by the great powers and often focused heavily on predominantly regional and divisive issues.

The division between India and other regional players emerged as a result of Nehru's quite different interpretation of what political independence meant in an international context. It was not simply independence from external interference but the freedom to realise a vision of an alternative world based on an Indian outlook and philosophy. This high ambition appeared to others as a reluctance on the part of the Indian leadership 'to step onto any podium smaller than the world stage', and spelt a decrease in India's popularity, as India became either a competitor or a hegemon in the eyes of less ambitious, confident or prestigious regional states.[115] India's pre-eminence in size, resources and experience as an independent state meant that no amount of sensitivity to the potential overbearing impact of its approach could shield it from accusations of domination. When the border war with China broke in 1962, India found little Afro–Asian support for its plight.

Non-proliferation

Nehru's deep reservations about nuclear weapons caused him to contest the great power norm of nuclear armament. Unsurprisingly, India was a pro-active advocate of disarmament throughout the 1950s and '60s. Nehru's formal advocacy against nuclear weapons commenced with the atomic bombing of Hiroshima and Nagasaki in 1945. In September 1945, he moved a resolution within the All India Congress Committee that deplored the atom bomb and what it stood for: 'the immoral and self-destructive elements of the present-day political, economic and spiritual structure of the world'.[116]

Nehru took up an activist stance in opposition to nuclear weapons soon after independence, viewing nuclear disarmament as a key step in the journey towards global peace. The official Indian position in this early phase was that disarmament would be possible only if there was agreement among the major powers but that it should also be essentially multilateral: disarmament negotiations should take place through the United Nations since it carried the principle responsibility for the maintenance of international peace and security.[117]

Following the *Fukuryu Maru* incident in early 1954, in which a Japanese fishing vessel was contaminated by radioactive fallout from the US testing of a hydrogen-bomb, the dangers of nuclear weapons testing generated sustained international controversy.[118] In April 1954, Nehru requested the United Nations to put the question of the cessation of nuclear weapons tests on its agenda.[119] Nehru's statement included a list of practical measures, the most ground-breaking of which was the 'standstill agreement' on explosions as an interim measure. This statement was the first UN document to mention the cessation of nuclear tests, and the first to separate testing from other arms control and disarmament measures. However, it initially drew little in the way of attention and consideration by the UN Disarmament Commission. Nehru also sought to take on an educating role. He asked the Indian Defence Science Organisation of the Government of India to compile an objective study of the consequences of the use of nuclear and other weapons of mass destruction in 1955. It was the first study of its kind. Through it, Nehru hoped to 'direct people's minds to the dreadful prospect of war in the nuclear age and to the danger of continuing nuclear test explosions'.[120] In the UN General Assembly's tenth session, India put forth a proposal on the question of 'Dissemination of information on the effects of atomic radiation and on the effects of experimental explosions of thermonuclear bombs'.[121] It found a response in the General Assembly resolution establishing the United Nations Scientific Committee on the Effects of Atomic Radiation in December 1955.[122] India had thus contributed to the mobilisation of world opinion on the harmful effects of nuclear testing.

A further Indian proposal was introduced to the Disarmament Commission in July 1956, which again demanded 'the cessation of all explosions and nuclear and other weapons of mass destruction' and urged the enlargement of the Commission to better represent the world both geographically and politically.[123] The message of this proposal was clear: the existing nuclear powers had proven themselves incapable of covering any ground in disarmament talks. Increased representation was not only desirable politically; it would likely be the only solution to the ongoing stalemate.

India continued to press for a ban on nuclear weapons testing. In 1957, at the twelfth session of the General Assembly, an Indian diplomatic team consisting of Krishna Menon and Arthur Samuel Lall proposed a commission of scientists from neutral countries to monitor and pronounce on cases of suspected weapons tests, in the event that a ban on weapons testing be set up. It was opposed by the United States and defeated when it came to the vote, but the resulting voting pattern on the Indian draft proposal was of significance: the total of the votes in favour of the proposal and the abstentions – which included Western European states – was higher than the votes against it. 'From now on', Lall later recounted, 'the weapons testing states had to take the opposition more seriously'.[124] India's and other countries' initiatives were beginning to make an impact.

The Disarmament Commission, as the main disarmament body outside of the General Assembly, was expanded in 1957 when fourteen members were added, including India, thanks to India's submission of an item entitled 'Expansion of the membership of the Disarmament Commission and of its Sub-Committee' during the twelfth session of the General Assembly.[125] It was enlarged again in 1958 to include all of the members of the United Nations, a step which reflected growing consensus that nuclear tests were a global concern. The major powers, however, continued to seek exclusive conference machinery linked to but not integral to the UN within which to discuss disarmament issues on an ad hoc basis. A tripartite Conference on the Discontinuance of Nuclear Weapon Tests, between the Soviet Union, the United States and the United Kingdom, commenced in October 1958 and ran until 1962, reviewed each year by the General Assembly. It achieved little progress. India remained shut out until its inclusion in the conference of the Eighteen Nation Disarmament Committee which ran from 1962 to 1968. It was this conference that would contribute significantly to early framings of the Nuclear Non-Proliferation Treaty (NPT), the final version of which India would reject, thereby precipitating India's indeterminate relationship to the nuclear non-proliferation regime that we see today.

Democracy and the liberal economic order

In the opening sections of this chapter, we argued that in terms of international norms, liberal democracy and capitalism stood dominant in the Nehru era, although they were challenged by communism. While much of India's approach to world politics entailed a spirit of rejection, on the issue of democracy India conformed to the democracy norm that was a key characteristic of the ideology of the Western camp.

Nehru's commitment to a democratic form of government centred both on his belief in its inherent value, and in the idea that 'a diverse, vast and divided country could not be held together and governed in any other way'.[126] British rule had established within India a relatively centralised state and had introduced 'proto-democratic' institutions and practices.[127] Nehru opted for the familiar Westminster parliamentary model, a federal polity with a strong centre and administratively autonomous states. He envisaged parliament as 'the central arena of political life providing an over-arching link between different linguistic and religious, racial, ethnic and other groups'.[128] Nehru played a vital role in India's democratic consolidation, fostering critique and opposition within the overwhelmingly dominant Congress party to compensate for the lack of any serious opposition outside the party itself; committing India to a regular course of, on the whole, free elections; adhering to constitutional rules and thereby institutionalising them; and committing the Indian polity to safeguarding minority rights and pursuing multi-religious nationhood.[129]

While India's initial choice of a democratic model of governance was not aimed at seeking status in and of itself, Indian diplomats would at times exploit India's democratic affinity with the United States. In 1948, for example, G. S. Bajpai, then secretary-general for external affairs, engaged in consultations with the United States over an Indian request for economic assistance. In reassuring his US interlocutors of India's true allegiance, despite its professed policy of non-alignment, he offered the reassurance that in the event that war with the Soviet Union broke out, 'India could only associate itself with those nations holding the same ideals of freedom and democracy'.[130] During the Nehru era, India did receive 'special acclaim' as the world's largest democracy, as a poor country and traditional society boldly seeking to achieve economic development along modern, democratic lines, and as a clear contrast to the authoritarian leaderships of some communist countries.[131] In effect, India could stand as a model for other countries. As the US National Security Council observed in 1959,

> The extent of India's development will have international ramifications … Asia and Africa will be watching and comparing what the Indian and Chinese regimes are achieving for their peoples, in terms of rapid industrialization, as well as in terms of the impact on human freedoms and living standards.[132]

Despite the deep differences between them over the Cold War, the United States nevertheless – and ironically on account of its Cold War strategy – did consider it important to provide economic assistance to India. As Chester Bowles, who became US ambassador to India in 1951, argued, the 'failure of Indian democracy would in all probability result in disaster substantially greater than Communist victory in China since Southeast Asia and the Middle East would become impossible to hold once India is lost'.[133]

India under Nehru did not, however, accept the economic dimensions of the US liberal doctrine by embracing capitalism. While inspired by the Soviet central planning of the 1920s and its objective of social equality, Nehru also did not embrace communist models of economics. A desire for economic self-sufficiency, fostered during the independence movement, was pursued as a foundation for India's economic policies after Independence. Nehru pursued a pathway of state-centred economic planning that sustained relatively stable economic growth on account of India's rapid industrialisation, recovery from the shrinkage of the economy under British rule, and the power and influence of Nehru and the Congress party in realising India's economic plans.[134]

Conclusion

The story of India's status seeking from 1947 to 1964 is a tale of a temporary rise in status, followed by collapse, primarily due to the absence of sufficient material power to defend India in the war against China in 1962. Above, we have seen the domestic, ideational roots of India's resistance to material capability and to the use of force as the core currency of international politics, and by extension, India's challenge to the standing of relative material capability as a central criterion for status. We also saw attempts at establishing a counter order. The global reach of India's status ambitions failed to gain acceptance from great powers, however, which did not see India's material capability as sufficient to warrant such a role; while weaker states were often alienated by India's global ambitions and perceived arrogance. Key lessons were learned as a result of India's failure to enhance its status through the acquisition of material capability and proximity to major powers. This led to the gradual adoption of these status criteria over subsequent decades, as we show in the next two chapters.

Notes

1 Keenleyside, T. A., 'The Inception of Indian Foreign Policy: The Non-Nehru Contribution', *South Asia: Journal of South Asian Studies*, vol. 4, no. 2 (1981), pp. 63–78.

2 Milner Jr, Murray, *Status and Sacredness: A General Theory of Status Relations and an Analysis of Indian Culture* (New York: Oxford University Press, 1994), p. 36.

3 Hassler, Sabine, *Reforming the UN Security Council Membership* (Abingdon and New York: Routledge, 2014).

4 Kristensen, Hans M. and Robert S. Norris, 'Global nuclear weapons inventories, 1945–2013', *Bulletin of the Atomic Scientists*, vol. 69, no. 5 (2013), pp. 75–81.

5 Buzan, Barry, *The United States and the Great Powers: World Politics in the Twenty-first Century* (Malden MA and Cambridge: Polity, 2004), p. 51.

6 Merrill, Dennis, *Bread and the Ballot*, (Chapel Hill: University of North Carolina Press, 1990), p. 3.

7 Merrill, *Bread and the Ballot*, p. 3.

8 Bromley, Simon, *American Power and the Prospects for International Order* (Cambridge: Polity Press, 2008), p. 82.

9 Merrill, *Bread and the Ballot*, p. 7.

10 Merrill, *Bread and the Ballot*, p. 35.

11 Buzan, *The United States and the Great Powers*.

12 Chaudhuri, Rudra, *Forged in Crisis: India and the United States since 1947* (London: Hurst, 2014), p. 31.

13 Nehru, Jawaharlal, *The Discovery of India* (New Delhi: Penguin, 2004 [1946]).

14 Parekh, Bhikhu, 'Nehru and the National Philosophy of India', *Economic and Political Weekly* (5 January 1991), pp. 35–48.

15 Parekh, 'Nehru and the National Philosophy of India'.

16 Naoroji's account of Britain's draining of India's wealth was particularly influential: Naoroji, Dadabhai, *Poverty and un-British rule in India* (London: Swan Sonnenschein, 1901).

17 Corbridge, Stuart and John Harriss, *Reinventing India: Liberalization, Hindu Nationalism and Popular Democracy* (Cambridge: Polity, 2000), p. 30.

18 World Bank, 'World Bank National Accounts Data, and OECD National Accounts Data Files', http://data.worldbank.org/indicator/NE. TRD.GNFS.ZS?end=2014&start=1964 (accessed on 5 December 2016).

19 Bhagwati, Jagdish N. and T. N. Srinivasan, *Foreign Trade Regimes and Economic Development: India* (Cambridge, MA: National Bureau of Economic Research, 1975), p. 5.

20 McMahon, Robert J., 'Food as a Diplomatic Weapon: The India Wheat Loan of 1951', *Pacific Historical Review*, vol. 56, no. 3 (1987), pp. 349–377.

21 Nehru, Jawaharlal, 'Speech to the US Congress', 13 October 1949, www. rediff.com/news/report/nehru-was-the-first-pm-to-address-the-us-congress/ 20160601.htm (accessed on 5 November 2016).

22 Nehru, 'Speech to the US Congress'.

23 Merrill, *Bread and the Ballot*, p. 1.

24 Boquerat, Gilles, *No Strings Attached? India's Policies and Foreign Aid, 1947–1966* (New Delhi: Manohar, 2003).

25 Cohen, Stephen P., *India: Emerging Power* (Washington, DC: Brookings Institution Press, 2001), p. 128.

26 Cohen, Stephen P. and Sunil Dasgupta, *Arming without Aiming: India's Military Modernization* (Washington, D.C.: Brookings Institution Press, 2010), p. 16.

27   Stockholm International Peace Research Institute, 'SIPRI Military Expenditure Database: Military expenditure data 1949–2015' (2016), www.sipri.org/databases/milex (accessed on 6 December 2016); Cohen and Dasgupta, *Arming without Aiming*, p. 16.

28   Charles Wolf, Jr, Gregory Hildebrandt, Michael Kennedy, Donald Putnam Henry, Katsuaki Terasawa, K. C. Yeh, Benjamin Zycher, Anil Bamezai and Toshiya Hayashi, *Long-Term Economic and Military Trends 1950– 2010: A Rand Note* (Santa Monica, CA: Rand Corporation, 1989), p. 17.

29   Cohen and Dasgupta, *Arming without Aiming*, pp. 2–3.

30   Cohen and Dasgupta, *Arming without Aiming*, p. 3.

31   Keenleyside, 'The Inception of Indian Foreign Policy', p. 69.

32   Keenleyside, T. A. 'Prelude to Power: The Meaning of Non-Alignment Before Indian Independence', *Pacific Affairs*, vol. 53, no. 3 (1980), p. 466.

33   Nehru, *The Discovery of India*; Keenleyside, 'Prelude to Power'.

34   Prasad, cited in: Keenleyside, 'Prelude to Power', p. 478.

35   Sullivan, Kate, 'Exceptionalism in Indian Diplomacy: The Origins of India's Moral Leadership Aspirations', *South Asia: Journal of South Asian Studies*, vol. 37, no. 4 (2014), pp. 640–655.

36   Constituent Assembly (Legislative) Debates (Internet Edition), vol. 17, 25 November 1948, p. 13 http://parliamentofindia.nic.in/ls/debates/vol7p13. htm (accessed on 15 August 2016).

37   Panikkar, K. M. *India and the Indian Ocean: An Essay on the Influence of Sea Power on Indian History* (London: Macmillan, 1945); Bajpai, G. S., 'India and the Balance of Power', *Indian Yearbook of International Affairs*, 1952, vol. 1 (1952), pp. 1–8.

38   Bajpai, 'India and the Balance of Power', p. 8.

39   Jawaharlal Nehru, cited in: Brown, Judith M., *Nehru: A Political Life* (New Haven, CT: Yale University Press, 2003), p. 268.

40   The five principles of *panchsheel* were 'mutual respect for each other's territorial integrity and sovereignty, mutual non-aggression, mutual non-interference in each other's internal affairs, equality and mutual benefit, and peaceful coexistence'. Brown, *Nehru: A Political Life*, p. 269.

41   Maxwell, Neville, 'Settlements and Disputes: China's Approach to Territorial Issues', *Economic and Political Weekly* (9 September 2006), pp. 3873–3881.

42   Lall, Arthur, *The Emergence of Modern India* (New York: Columbia University Press, 1981).

43   Ministry of External Affairs, *Report of the Committee on the Indian Foreign Service* (Delhi: Ministry of External Affairs, 1966), p. 10.

44   Brecher, Michael, *India and World Politics: Krishna Menon's View of the World* (London: Oxford University Press, 1968), pp. 231–232, 312–314.

45   Ghatate, N. M., 'Disarmament Logic: Learning from Nehru's Nuclear Vision', *Times of India*, 18 September 1998, p. 12.

46   Kapur, Ashok, *India's Nuclear Option* (New York: Praeger, 1976), pp. 193–194.

47   Constituent Assembly (Legislative) Debates vol. V, pp. 3315–3334.

48   Constituent Assembly (Legislative) Debates vol. V, p. 3315.

49   Constituent Assembly (Legislative) Debates vol. V, p. 3333–3334.

50   Nehru, cited in: Mirichandani, G. G., *India's Nuclear Dilemma* (New Delhi: Popular Book Services, 1968), p. 6.

51 Keenleyside, 'Prelude to Power', pp. 461–483.
52 On becoming head of the Interim Government in 1946.
53 Nehru, Jawaharlal, 'Free India's Role in World Affairs', in Jawaharlal Nehru, *Selected Works of Jawaharlal Nehru: Second Series*, vol. I (New Delhi: Oxford University Press, 1984), p. 404.
54 Nehru, Jawaharlal, *Letters to Chief Ministers, vol. 1, 1947–1949* (Oxford: Oxford University Press, 1990), p. 94.
55 Kochanek, S. A., 'India's Changing Role in the United Nations', *Pacific Affairs*, vol. 53, no. 1 (1980), pp. 49–50.
56 Nehru, *Letters to Chief Ministers, vol. 1*, p. 61.
57 Ibid., p. 61.
58 Ibid., pp. 69–70.
59 Ibid., pp. 80–81.
60 Khan, Mohammed Ayub, 'The Pakistan-American Alliance: Stresses and Strains', *Foreign Affairs*, vol. 42, no. 2 (1964), pp. 195–209.
61 Mastny, Vojtech, 'The Soviet Union's Partnership with India', *Journal of Cold War Studies*, vol. 12, no. 3 (Summer 2010), p. 52; Chari, 'Indo-Soviet Military Cooperation', p. 232.
62 The United States, France, Great Britain, New Zealand, Australia, the Philippines, Thailand and Pakistan formed SEATO in 1954.
63 CENTO was established in 1955 by Iran, Iraq, Pakistan, Turkey, and the United Kingdom. Although the United States did not join, the organisation was intended to contain the Soviet Union to its southwest and its establishment was driven by the Anglo–US alliance.
64 Keenleyside, 'Prelude to Power', p. 461.
65 Brecher, Michael, 'Non-alignment Under Stress: The West and the India-China Border War', *Pacific Affairs,* vol. 52, no. 4 (Winter 1979–1980), pp. 612–630.
66 Brecher, 'Non-alignment Under Stress', p. 617.
67 Brecher, 'Non-alignment Under Stress'.
68 Ibid., p. 626; Bowles, Chester, 'America and Russia in India', *Foreign Affairs*, vol. 49, no. 4 (July 1971), p. 640.
69 Brecher, 'Non-alignment Under Stress'.
70 Bowles, 'America and Russia in India', p. 642.
71 Chari, 'Indo-Soviet Military Cooperation', p. 234.
72 Ibid., p. 237.
73 Brecher, 'Non-alignment Under Stress', pp. 628–629.
74 Harrison, Selig, 'Troubled India and Her Neighbours', *Foreign Affairs*, vol. 43, no. 2 (January 1965), p. 326.
75 Milner, *Status and Sacredness*, p. 36.
76 Nehru, *Letters to Chief Ministers, vol. 1*, pp. 44–45.
77 Keenleyside, 'The Inception of Indian Foreign Policy'.
78 Rubinoff, Arthur G., 'The Multilateral Imperative in India's Foreign Policy', *The Round Table*, no. 319 (1991), p. 314.
79 Karunakaran, K. P., *India in World Affairs: August 1947–January 1950* (Calcutta: Oxford University Press, 1952), p. 84–85.
80 Nehru, Jawaharlal, *Speeches, vol. 1: 1946–1949* (New Delhi: Ministry of Information and Broadcasting, 1967), p. 300.
81 Rubinoff, 'The Multilateral Imperative', p. 317.
82 Ibid.

83   Abraham, 'From Bandung to NAM', p. 202.
84   Nehru, cited in: Karunakaran, *India in World Affairs*, p. 88.
85   Nehru, Jawaharlal, *Speeches, vol. 1: 1946–1949* (New Delhi: Ministry of Information and Broadcasting, 1967), p. 255.
86   Mansergh, Nicholas, 'Review: India in World Affairs', *International Affairs*, vol. 29, no. 4 (1953), p. 524.
87   Dayal, Rajeshwar, *A Life of Our Times* (London: Sangam, 1998), p. 204.
88   Arnold, Guy, *Historical Dictionary of the Non-Aligned and Third World* (Lanham, MD: Scarecrow Press, 2006), p. 11.
89   Dayal, *A Life of Our Times*, p. 206.
90   Ibid., p. 205.
91   Ibid., pp. 205–206.
92   Jha, Chandra Shekhar, *From Bandung to Tashkent: Glimpses of India's foreign policy* (Delhi: Sangam Books, 1983), p. 62; Reid, Anthony, 'The Bandung Conference and Southeast Asian Regionalism', in See Seng Tan and Amitav Acharaya, eds, *Bandung Revisited: The Legacy of the Asian-African Conference for International Order* (Singapore: NUS Press, 2008), p. 25.
93   Brecher, Michael, *Nehru: A Political Biography (Abridged Edition)* (Boston: Beacon Press, 1959), p. 227.
94   Gopal, Sarvepalli, *Jawaharlal Nehru: A Biography (Abridged Edition)* (New Delhi: Oxford University Press, 1989), p. 284.
95   Tyabji, Badr-ud-din, *Memoirs of an Egoist, Volume One: 1907–1956* (New Delhi: Roli, 1988), p. 319.
96   Tyabji, *Memoirs of an Egoist*, p. 319.
97   Gopal, *Jawaharlal Nehru*, p. 286.
98   Jha, *From Bandung to Tashkent*, p. 70.
99   Ibid.
100 Gopal, *Jawaharlal Nehru*, p. 286.
101 Abraham, 'From Bandung to NAM', p. 207.
102 Reid, 'The Bandung Conference', p. 24.
103 Romulo, cited in: Reid, 'The Bandung Conference', p. 24.
104 Tyabji, *Memoirs of an Egoist*, p. 318.
105 Ibid., p. 325.
106 Ibid., p. 318.
107 Jha, *From Bandung to Tashkent*, p. 168.
108 Reid, 'The Bandung Conference', p. 25.
109 Willetts, Peter, *The Non-Aligned Movement. The Origins of a Third World Alliance* (London: Frances Pinter, 1978), p. 11.
110 Gopal, *Jawaharlal Nehru*, p. 407.
111 Gopal, *Jawaharlal Nehru*, p. 407.
112 Rubinoff, 'The Multilateral Imperative', pp. 321–322.
113 Gopal, *Jawaharlal Nehru*, p. 407.
114 Ibid., p. 408.
115 Willets, *The Non-Aligned Movement*, p. 12.
116 Cited in: Mirichandani, *India's Nuclear Dilemma*, p. 5.
117 Speech by Krishna Menon, 8 April 1953, cited in: Arora, K. C., *V. K. Krishna Menon: A Biography* (New Delhi: Sanchar Publishing House, 1998), p. 186.
118 Jain, Jagdish P., *India and Disarmament*, (New Delhi: Radiant, 1974), p. 70; Foster, John Bellamy, *The Ecological Revolution: Making Peace with the Planet* (New York: Monthly Review Press, 2009), p. 73.

119 Lall, Arthur S., *Negotiating Disarmament: The Eighteen Nation Disarmament Conference: The First Two Years, 1962–64* (Ithaca, NY: Cornell University Center for International Studies, 1964), p. 2.
120 Nehru, 'Foreword', in Kothari, D. S., *Nuclear Explosions and their Effects* (Delhi: Ministry of Information and Broadcasting, Government of India, 1956), p. v.
121 United Nations, *The United Nations and Disarmament 1945–70* (New York: United Nations, 1970), p. 193; U.N. Doc. A/C.1/L.239 and Add.1.
122 Myrdal, Alva, *The Game of Disarmament: How the United States and Russia Run the Arms Race* (New York: Pantheon Books, 1976), pp. 85–86.
123 United Nations, *The United Nations and Disarmament*, pp. 665–667; U.N. Doc. DC/98 July 31, 1956.
124 Lall, *The Emergence of Modern India*, p. 137.
125 United Nations, *The United Nations and Disarmament 1945–70*, p. 70.
126 Parekh, 'Nehru and the National Philosophy of India', p. 36.
127 Kohli, Atul, 'Introduction', in Atul Kohli, ed., *The Success of India's Democracy* (Cambridge: Cambridge University Press), p. 18.
128 Parekh, 'Nehru and the National Philosophy of India', p. 36.
129 Varshney, Ashutosh, *Battles Half Won: India's Improbable Democracy* (New Delhi: Penguin, 2013), pp. 26–29.
130 G. S. Bajpai, cited in: Merrill, Dennis, 'Indo-American Relations, 1947–50: A Missed Opportunity in Asia', *Diplomatic History*, vol. 11, no. 3 (1987), p. 208.
131 Merrill, *Bread and the Ballot*, pp. 2–3.
132 National Security Council, cited in: Merrill, *Bread and the Ballot*, p. 5.
133 Bowles, cited in: Das, Ajaya Kumar, 'India–US Relations: Assessing India's Soft Power', Ph.D. dissertation, Nanyang Technological University, Singapore, 2015, p. 108.
134 Sibal, D. Rajeev, 'The Untold Story of India's Economy', in *India: The Next Superpower* (London: London School of Economics, 2012), pp. 17–22.

3 Incipient power, limited status in the post-Nehru era (1964–1991)

Introduction

This chapter explores India's attempts at seeking status during the period following the death of Jawaharlal Nehru, in 1964, up until the end of the Cold War period, in 1990. In the previous chapter we showed how, under Nehru's leadership, India rejected the dominant associational sources of status – material attributes and proximity to dominant powers – to the detriment of Indian security *and* status. In the post-Nehru era, we find distinct changes in India's quest for both security and status. First, the material instruments of power, traditionally viewed as symbols of status but relatively neglected by Nehru, received close attention. Nonetheless, India did not pursue the development of nuclear weapons despite serious perceptions of a Chinese nuclear threat from 1964. Alongside the rapid acquisition of military power, New Delhi began to exercise this power forcefully through regional interventions, gaining a degree of prestige but also stoking fears about a future of Indian hegemony in the region. Second, Nehru had avoided economic and strategic proximity to the major powers except during the last phase of his premiership when he was compelled to seek US assistance amidst the war with China. Post-Nehru leaders continued with his emphasis on economic self-sufficiency and non-alignment, but came to rely on both the United States and the Soviet Union on critically important economic and strategic issues.

With regard to the normative sources of status, India's counter-order agenda continued. An ongoing rejection of great power politics and Cold War dynamics was reflected in Indian efforts at strengthening and securing the future of the Non-Aligned Movement (NAM) in the 1960s and again in the early 1980s; in Prime Minister Indira Gandhi's incipient environmental activism; and in India's contributions to the establishment of the United Nations Conference on Trade and Development and the

Group of 77. India challenged the nascent non-proliferation regime, first by refusing to sign the Nuclear Non-Proliferation Treaty (NPT) in 1968, and then by conducting a nuclear explosion in 1974. In an unexpected way, however, India also conformed to non-proliferation norms by not opting to develop a nuclear arsenal. Domestically, the Indian polity survived internal stress in the mid-1970s and would ultimately preserve its reputation as the world's largest democracy. Overall, India's quest for status through normative innovation continued, but, in contrast to the Nehru era, this quest was accompanied by the pursuit of material power as a means to security.

Dominant material associations and international norms

The period under discussion continued to be dominated globally by the Cold War and its material and normative underpinnings. The predominant feature in the material dimension was the nuclear arms race between the United States and the Soviet Union, which made the commonplace term 'superpower' seem apposite. At its peak in 1986, the global nuclear inventory totalled 64,449 nuclear warheads, of which well over 63,476 were in the possession of the United States and the Soviet Union.[1] In this context, India's minimalist approach to nuclear weapons during this period is significant. The difficulties faced by the dominant powers in translating military power into strategic gains were underlined not only by the essential non-usability of nuclear weapons, but by their failures even with conventional weapons. The United States had to retreat from a costly war in Vietnam, while the Soviet Union was compelled to do the same in Afghanistan. India, which reversed its neglect of conventional military power, also ran into similar difficulties in its bid to exercise military control over Sri Lanka. Still, the currency of military power remained strong and even major setbacks did not devalue it.

Economic power, too, was important, but its distribution was less lopsided. To be sure, the United States had emerged as the unchallenged economic power in the aftermath of World War II, but by the 1980s much had changed. Europe had recovered, Japan was a powerful competitor, and the Asian 'tigers' – Hong Kong, Singapore, South Korea and Taiwan – were on the ascendant, resulting in the relative decline of the United States.[2] The utility of economic power as an instrument of national policy, though, was constrained by the rapid integration of the world economy, which led to increasing interdependence and precluded a repeat of the mercantilist trade wars that had occurred in earlier times.[3] The success stories were of those states that opted for close relationships with the centres of power. But India, which kept a distance from the increasingly integrated world economy, was not a significant player.

The predominant norms of the era were shaped by the United States, though the Soviet Union tried – with limited success – to create its own. A norm that continued from the Nehru era was related to Cold War power politics: all states were expected to range themselves on one side or the other. The separation of France from the North Atlantic Treaty Organization and of China from the Soviet bloc in the 1960s was a challenge to Washington and Moscow, but did not seriously alter Cold War dynamics. Concomitantly, all states were expected to attach themselves to the economic arrangements – capitalist or socialist – adopted by the two blocs. Many developing countries were unwilling to abide by this global division. During this period, a world-spanning effort to change both political and economic structures achieved some momentum through the Non-Aligned Movement and the Group of 77 (G77) developing economies respectively. India's leading role in both is discussed below.

A third major norm that emerged at this time was that of nuclear non-proliferation. Here too there was a global divide, but a very different one. The new divide was between the existing nuclear powers and the rest. The Nuclear Non-Proliferation Treaty (NPT), opened for signature in 1968 and in force from 1970, recognised the former as legitimate possessors of nuclear weapons and the latter as not entitled to the same. On this issue, the United States and the Soviet Union stood together to prevent the spread of nuclear armaments. India, though hesitating to pursue the nuclear option even after China had tested the bomb in 1964, strongly resisted the NPT and the regime that was constructed around it.

Associational status seeking in the post-Nehru era

Material attributes

The shock of India's defeat in 1962 galvanised Indian elites into rethinking a key aspect of their approach to international politics. This was reflected in partial but important changes in India's approach to both security and status. In terms of associations with material power, Nehru's successors dropped his reluctance to develop military power and began a sustained effort to build the armed forces. The pace of economic growth remained sluggish till the mid-1970s, which meant that India at times faced severe difficulties, particularly with respect to the availability of food in the mid-1960s. Unsurprisingly, we find a surge in military spending immediately after the 1962 war. But the growth of a nuclear capability, though launched shortly after Nehru's death in 1964, remained slow, with limited interest in nuclear weapons development even after the threshold was crossed in 1974. India also attempted to sustain a distant relationship with the global economy and the major powers, but without great success. Nevertheless, India's strategic profile grew steadily, first to that of a dominant player in the Subcontinent and gradually to a major power in the Indian Ocean region. By the 1980s, India had attained the stature of a 'regional superpower'.[4] Observers noted a 'retreat from idealism' and a more hard-headed approach to foreign policy, particularly within India's region. Broadly, however, the Indian vision of an alternative possible world order continued through India's efforts at normative status-seeking, as we show below.[5]

Economic power

Perhaps the key challenge facing India in the post-Nehru era was what Indira Gandhi – Jawaharlal Nehru's daughter and India's prime minister from 1966 to 1977 and 1980 to 1984 – described as the need to 'reconcile the competing claims of development and defence'.[6] India had suffered not only a loss to China in the 1962 war, but had also been required to fight a war with Pakistan in 1965.

The challenge was a politically difficult one given the context of India's growing aggregate population living under the poverty line. Independence had brought a 'revolution of rising expectations'[7] that – in the absence of adequate growth and distribution – had the potential to, and periodically did, produce rising frustrations and societal turbulence. Indira Gandhi's accession to power in 1966 coincided with a major drought and a consequent food crisis which forced India to depend on the United States for food aid. This dependence created a poor image of an impoverished, aid-dependent country. India struggled again with drought in 1972–1973, was burdened with refugee relief following the 1971 war with Pakistan, and experienced food shortages and rising prices in response to the 1973 global oil crisis.[8]

As we showed in the previous chapter, the growth of the economy was slow under Nehru's state-dominated and autarkic 'mixed economy'. As India struggled with investment and technology, its GDP grew slowly from $57.40 billion in 1964 to $326.60 billion in 1990.[9] The so-called 'Hindu rate of growth' (3.4 per cent) that broadly prevailed between 1956 and 1974 was, to be sure, interspersed with periods of faster growth.[10] Ganguly and Mukherjee identify the subsequent period from 1974 to 1991 as one of faster growth (over 5 per cent), while McCartney finds accelerated growth during the period from 1979/80 to 1991.[11] But per capita GDP growth lagged, rising from $117.80 in 1964 to $375.20 in 1990 – far slower than the experience of other major developing countries during the same period, such as Brazil (from $259.50 to $3,071.60) and Mexico (from $463.90 to $3,068.70).[12]

The upshot was that India's status remained low from the economic standpoint. The pace of economic growth was sluggish till the mid-1970s, which meant that India at times faced severe difficulties. Slow growth in turn constrained military spending. However, this did not stop India from making status gains in the military-strategic realm.

Military power

Following the 1962 catastrophe, Nehru and his successors relinquished their former reluctance to invest in military power and began a sustained effort to build the armed forces. The drive for a stronger military was immediately reflected in higher defence spending. Chari describes how India's post-1962 defence policy framework was built on three pillars:

> First, a military build-up was effected through an increase in force levels; existing equipment deficiencies were made up and, simultaneously, equipment modernized. Second, reliance on external supplies was minimized as much as possible, and restricted to the import of advanced types of weaponry. Third, greater emphasis was laid on indigenous production to achieve progressively higher levels of self-reliance and self-sufficiency.[13]

As mentioned, the war with China triggered faster military modernisation. Military expenditure, which stood at $4.27 billion in 1962, jumped by over 50 per cent to $6.83 billion in 1964, while military spending as a proportion of GDP shot up from 2.7 per cent in 1962 to 4 per cent the following year and held steady at 3.8 per cent in 1964.[14] The defence budget would fall somewhat in the late 1960s and during the 1970s due to economic stagnation.[15] In 1990, however, it stood at 3.2 per cent, with actual spending, spurred by the higher rate of growth, reaching a substantial $18.54 billion.[16] In parallel, military capital stocks (of weapons and structures) grew five-fold from $9 billion in 1960 to $42 billion in 1990.[17] By 1990, India was the seventh highest military spender in the world despite its relatively slow growth.[18]

The lack of a significant domestic armaments production industry led India to look overseas for major acquisitions. The United States was not a source owing to political differences, but Moscow was quick to step in with combat aircraft, naval vessels and tanks, while major purchases were also made from Britain (combat aircraft), France (combat aircraft), Sweden (field guns) and West Germany (submarines). Moreover, the Indian military began building force projection capabilities. As one contemporary commentator observed, with its long-range armour-lifting Il-76 aircraft, India had 'the heaviest combat airlift of any air force outside the United States Air Force or the Soviet Air Force'.[19] India's growing military capacity was underlined by two major acquisitions from the Soviet Union in the late 1980s: TU142M long-range maritime reconnaissance and anti-submarine warfare aircraft, and a leased nuclear-powered submarine. These acquisitions signalled India's ambitions for a major role in the Indian Ocean.

In addition to the new imperative to acquire military power, the 1962 war also had effects on Indian thinking on the link between military power and India's status. There was recognition that a refusal to spend on defence – even though there was limited foreign exchange to do so – had fundamentally undermined Indian aspirations to take leadership on, and accrue status from, the fostering of a peaceful and more equitable world order. Arthur Samuel Lall, an Indian diplomat in the 1950s and early 1960s, later explained how India's failure to raise its military profile had resulted in 'exclusion from the councils of the great to which it was entitled not only because of its population but also because it has been for several millennia among the world's major civilisations'.[20] A discourse emerged that saw international status for India as dependent on a mix of principle and material power.[21] The task was to test the claim that G. S. Bajpai had made back in 1952 – that the acquisition of material power would not eclipse India's capacity for moral leadership, and was indeed essential for its projection.[22]

Indira Gandhi came to play a vital role in India's acquisition of military and economic power. Her interest was in 'possessing tangible attributes of power'.[23] While she emphasised that '[w]e want India to be self-reliant and to strengthen its independence so that it cannot be pressurized by anybody', she also claimed that India's foreign policy was 'motivated to defend autonomy rather than extend power'.[24] Nonetheless, as will be shown later, the Indian conception of power also involved an increasing tendency to project it through external interventions, some unwelcome.

Nuclear power

While India moved ahead with the acquisition of conventional military power, its leaders in the post-Nehru era remained ambivalent about nuclear weapons.[25] Two years after defeating India in a conventional war, China tested its first nuclear weapon in 1964. In December 1965, Nehru's successor Lal Bahadur Shastri, prime minister from 1964 to 1966, responded by approving the Subterranean Nuclear Explosion Project, with the proviso that the project should stop short of actually building the bomb.[26] Indira Gandhi subsequently authorised the conduct of a single nuclear explosion in 1974, but did not opt to build an arsenal. Certainly, a strategic motive for the 1974 test can be deduced. India had experienced a symbolic nuclear threat during the December 1971 war with Pakistan when the Nixon administration sent the nuclear-armed US Seventh Fleet into the Bay of Bengal to warn India and the Soviet Union against contemplating – in US Secretary of State Henry Kissinger's words – the 'eventual disintegration' of Pakistan.[27] In this sense, Indira Gandhi may have carried out the test at least partly as a symbolic response.

However, the 1974 explosion cannot be viewed in isolation from India's position with regard to a newly consolidating nuclear non-proliferation order centred on the NPT. Even while Indian diplomats had actively championed the establishment of an international instrument to curb the proliferation of nuclear weapons, what they had intended was a universal agreement that would also establish a mechanism for nuclear disarmament, not a treaty that effectively privileged the interests and permitted the maintenance of the nuclear weapons status of the nuclear powers. The United States, the United Kingdom, and the Soviet Union, all of whom would come to be recognised Nuclear-Weapon States according to the terms of the Treaty, immediately ratified the NPT in 1968. India resisted signing then, and has done so ever since. In the words of M. C. Chagla, India's external affairs minister from 1966 to 1967, 'the nuclear powers were only interested in maintaining their own nuclear supremacy and monopoly'.[28] In this context, the 1974 test can be read as an act of defiance against emerging non-proliferation norms, and we reinforce this argument below. While voices in favour of India's transition to the rank of a nuclear weapons power existed, especially among the Jana Sangh Party, with its largely Hindu nationalist tilt, and the conservative Swatantra Party, a shift to weaponisation was not a serious consideration for the majority of the political and bureaucratic elite.[29]

Beyond this, however, the personal convictions of both Indira and Rajiv Gandhi appear to have been at the root of their respective unwillingness to go further and begin building an arsenal. Indira is reported to have told her chief scientific advisor V. S. Arunachalam that she was 'basically against weapons of mass destruction'.[30] The nuclear option was nevertheless opened wider: in July 1983, she launched the Integrated Guided Missile Development Programme, which would later become the centrepiece of India's nuclear arsenal. Rajiv was similarly indecisive. According to Arunachalam, he was 'genuinely against the bomb', but 'did not want India to be found wanting in a crisis either'.[31] Though he did sanction the making of nuclear weapons in 1989, this order was kept covert and had no bearing on India's status as a nuclear-armed state. The acquisition of nuclear capability under both Indira and Rajiv appeared aimed – reluctantly – at security. But also, as we show below, it sought to challenge a nuclear order that, despite Indian efforts within disarmament forums, continued to view nuclear weapons as a source of status, and positioned India within the lower status tier of states that chose to forgo nuclear weapons. The long-term result of India's cautious quest for nuclear security, and the ultimate solution to India's lower status in the nuclear order, was India's nuclear weaponisation in 1998, as we argue in the next chapter.

Relations with the dominant powers

India's economic policy during the 1960s and after continued along the autarkic lines set by Nehru. But autonomy was hard to sustain. Foreign trade in 1964 amounted to only 9 per cent of GDP and, by 1990, was still one of the lowest in the world at 15 per cent.[32] By the early 1960s, India emerged as 'the world's leading recipient of American economic aid'.[33] President Lyndon Johnson, exasperated by Indian criticism of the American war in Vietnam, deliberately delayed the despatch of food-carrying ships until the last moment in what was known as the 'short tether' policy.[34] Indira Gandhi's response was a stronger determination to avoid dependence and to apply populist left-leaning policies (although she also aimed at strengthening her political position at home).[35] The largest private banks were nationalised, big business controlled by the 1969 Monopolies and Restrictive Trade Practices Act, and foreign investment restricted under the 1973 Foreign Exchange Regulation Act. The aim was to avoid dependency on foreign capital, which was viewed with suspicion as 'neo-colonial' and exploitative.

Unfortunately, the objective of economic self-sufficiency was harder to achieve than anticipated. The problem of food production was only alleviated by cooperation with the United States to employ modern technologies for the increase of agricultural production in what came to be known as the 'green revolution'.[36] In 1970, Indira Gandhi urged India's public and private sectors to 'rely more and more on our own machinery and technical know-how' since 'excessive reliance on [foreign collaboration] has induced a state of mind which inhibits the development of our own technological skills and managerial talents'.[37] Reemphasising the need for self-sufficiency, she stressed, how 'it would be folly to forget that a nation's strength ultimately consists in what it can do on its own and not in what it can borrow from others'.[38] After India's 1971 war with Pakistan, the United States withdrew aid from India to signal US disapproval of India's actions, and the World Bank took over as a major lender.

Meanwhile, overall growth remained modest. In the global context, India's position was unenviable. World GDP rose by 1,253 per cent between 1964 and 1990, whereas India's GDP in the same period grew by just 568 per cent, which meant that the Indian economy was effectively falling behind.[39] Even as growth picked up in the 1980s, the vulnerability of the economy increased, bringing a debt crisis in 1991 that compelled drastic policy changes (discussed in the next chapter). Overall, India's effort to attain economic security through self-sufficiency was a signal failure.

In the realm of strategic politics, the experience was less painful, although the results were mixed. Indira Gandhi and her successors carried forward Nehru's non-alignment baton and continued to try and play a leadership role within the Non-Aligned Movement, a theme we elaborate upon below. However, India's temporary proximity to the United States through Nehru's acceptance of US military assistance in 1962, and subsequent growing proximity to the Soviet Union through the sourcing of military assets and supplies, led to outside scepticism surrounding India's national policy of non-alignment. India's tilt toward the Soviet Union became yet more visible in 1971, when India signed the Indo–Soviet Treaty of Peace, Friendship and Cooperation – a virtual defence pact – with the Soviet Union. Article IX of the Treaty incorporated a provision for 'consultations' and for 'appropriate effective measures to ensure peace and the security of their countries', which implied possible military action.[40] The Treaty was signed primarily to counter a sense of isolation in the face of growing warmth between Washington, Beijing and Islamabad. However, in the context of the 1971 crisis in East Pakistan, which would lead to India's third war with Pakistan, it appeared to allow the possibility of Soviet intervention if a foreign power – either China or the United States – intervened militarily in Pakistan's favour. However, the Treaty can be read as only obliquely strategic. In contrast to the extensive defence cooperation between India and the United States today, Indo–Soviet strategic relations were largely composed of weapons supplies and were otherwise far less close in terms of joint activities such as strategic dialogues, military exercises and logistics sharing.

The desire to remain insulated from great power influence remained strong in India. The events of both 1962 and 1971 alike thus spelt crises in India's application of the policy of non-alignment, and Indian leaders and scholars alike sought to redefine the concept to allow for 'military assistance', 'equal proximity rather than equal distance from the superpowers' and 'virtual military alliance'.[41] By the late 1980s, while material gains had begun to enhance India's status, India was unavoidably and deeply engaged with both of the dominant powers, whether economically or strategically. Proximity to the centres of power perhaps did not bring status in the post-Nehru era, but India's intensifying engagements laid the foundation for stronger relations with major powers in the 1990s and beyond that, as we discuss in the next chapter, would later bring considerable status benefits.

Normative status seeking in the post-Nehru era

During the post-Nehru period, India's relationship with dominant global norms showed a mixed record. On the one hand, Indian leaders continued to resist the capitalist world economy, the prevailing Cold War norm of aligning with one of the two blocs, and the nuclear non-proliferation regime. On the other hand, besides embracing (conventional) military power, India began to emulate the strategic behaviour that was the norm for the dominant powers, assigning itself the role of maintaining regional order.

Responses to dominant global norms

India's crushing loss of status following the military defeat to China in 1962 led to a growing awareness among Indian political leaders that international influence could not follow without a foundation of strength. As we have outlined above, India shifted toward conformity with one key source of associational status, that of material capability. However, where normative sources of status were concerned, India's prior attempts at innovation persisted through a continued rejection of the Cold War power struggle and India's self-projection as the leader of 'alternative' groupings.

Indian counter-order leadership shone particularly at four key moments in the post-Nehru era. First, India was able to restore some of its prestige as a leader of the Third World through a successful Second Non-Aligned summit held in Cairo in October 1964 that excluded China and Pakistan and saw membership more than double: twenty-nine countries were in attendance. Rather than an obvious successor to the first Non-Aligned Summit in Belgrade (1961), Cairo was in fact the outcome of a bitterly fought competition between a 'second Bandung' and a 'second Belgrade'. Indonesia's President Sukarno had been keen to repeat the success both of the Bandung conference itself and of Indonesia's centrality in the proceedings. After a failed attempt at convening a second Afro–Asian conference in March 1961 (a year that became dominated by the first Non-Aligned conference at Belgrade[42]), Sukarno tried again in March 1964, inviting nineteen countries to send representatives to Jakarta to consider planning for a tenth-anniversary follow-up Afro–Asian conference to be held in 1965.[43] He had, however, consulted with only one of the other four Colombo Powers who had co-sponsored the 1955 conference, and that country was not India.[44] Instead, the planning was being undertaken by Indonesia, China and Pakistan, a triad that from all angles could be nothing but anti-Indian. China and India had clashed momentously in the 1962 border war. Pakistan was under the military rule of President Ayub Khan and was in close collaboration with China. Sukarno had 'developed a strange allergy to Nehru and India' and 'anti-India feelings' had grown in Indonesia.[45] As a show of Afro–Asian solidarity, the conference had little hope of success, but as a distraction from the Second Non-Aligned Summit, planned for October 1964, it contained more than an element of anti-Indian potency. From an Indian perspective, Sukarno's plan for a second Bandung heralded disaster, uniting three of India's adversaries in an unstable Afro–Asian climate in which India had lost a great deal of prestige, not least as a result of the ruinous losses in the border war with China.

India solved the problem with simple sabotage.[46] At preparatory conferences in Jakarta in 1964 and again in Algiers in 1965, India's representative, Chandra Shekhar Jha 'became deeply involved in the question of who should be invited' to the second Afro–Asian conference.[47] The controversial suggestion of the Soviet Union as a participant generated serious conflict with China. Here was masterful diplomacy at work: India had placed an insurmountable hurdle in the way of the future of the Afro–Asian conference, packaged it in an apparently benevolent and well-argued proposal, and responded to the ensuing anger from China, especially, in measured and conciliatory tones. The conference was postponed, postponed again and ultimately never convened, leaving the Indian delegation – according to Jha, at least – 'in the limelight', having shown itself 'still a force to be reckoned with in the Asian-African world'.[48]

The potency of Afro–Asian solidarity was revealed as diminished, a clear success for India, since the forum that survived – the Non-Aligned

Movement – had a broad international agenda rather than a narrow anti-colonial one and offered a platform for India to approach global problems with regional support. In terms of membership, too, the Non-Aligned grouping of states had a broader geographical representation, and, through its careful membership criteria, was less at risk – but by no means entirely insulated, as we shall see – from inside manipulation by states that were part of military pacts or alliances with either of the Cold War rivals. Within the NAM, India was also insulated from the risk of being upstaged by China or undermined by Pakistan. Moreover, in the choice between an 'association with a group identified with the politics of racial affiliation' and 'a heterogeneous group identified around the critique of prevailing international order', the latter had triumphed.[49] By resonating, in ideational terms, more closely with Indian notions of non-alignment, and by offering a more prominent place on the world stage, India's role in the Non-Aligned Movement held greater promise on a pathway to status.

A second boost to India's capacity for counter-order leadership came on the back of the NAM, which, beyond the summit meetings, also emerged as a practical mode of adopting collective stances on issues within the United Nations. A broad community of states arose around trade and economic development issues and a common desire to negotiate a restructuring of the international economic order. Although this grouping was not identical to the NAM, it was largely contiguous, and it grew to play a major role in creating a space for a collective international development agenda at the centre of the global agenda.[50] This broad platform of developing countries comprising Asian, African and Latin American countries united under the banner of the Group of 77 (G77) was established on 15 June 1964 by seventy-seven developing countries in the context of the first session of the United Nations Conference on Trade and Development (UNCTAD) in Geneva. As one of the originators of the idea of UNCTAD, India was thus a key force in attempting to drive forward the economic demands of developing states through the G77. Momentum for such a restructuring was boosted by the oil crisis of 1973, in which Arab members of the Organization of Petroleum Exporting Countries (OPEC) made cuts in oil production and banned petroleum exports to the United States and other states that offered support to Israel during the 1973 Arab-Israeli War. The programme for a New International Economic Order (NIEO) was initiated at the fourth Non-Aligned summit at Algiers in 1973, and later adopted by the UN General Assembly in early 1974.[51]

Thus, while the NAM, as a social movement of non-aligned nations, initially took form as part of a wider political strategy in the early

1960s to guard against foreign intervention in Africa and Asia, in the 1970s it was midwife to a collective economic movement of Third World countries, fighting for a NIEO based on equality and justice. The central premise of the group's thinking at the time was that the post-colonial era had brought a new form of structural inequality: despite formal independence, the countries of the 'South' were still dominated by the rich 'North' by means of unequal terms of trade. With India playing a prominent role, the countries of the South demanded more equitable terms of trade and higher levels of aid from the developed nations while also attempting to expand South–South trade.[52] Yet, while India was one of the originators of the idea of UNCTAD, it 'did not occupy a leading place in negotiations between the industrialised North and the developing South when they took on a confrontationist tone'.[53] Instead, India assumed the role of mediator, urging moderation among radical members of the South and the continuation of dialogue on the part of the North. This position again underscored an Indian desire to function as a pivotal intermediary on major world economic issues, rather than to adopt wholesale common cause with other developing countries and compromise its wider interests and aspirations.[54] Such a position carved out an elevated space for India, apart from the G77, yet it also left India's options open when the debt crisis of the 1980s hit, and the world economic order moved decisively against the demands and aspirations embodied within calls for a NIEO.[55]

A third key episode of Indian counter-order leadership took shape at the UN Conference on the Human Environment held in Stockholm in June 1972, the first ever major international conference on international environmental issues.[56] Indira Gandhi attended as the lone head of government apart from the host nation's prime minister, Olof Palme. Her address to the Stockholm plenary on 14 June 1972 captured international attention. Framing environmental degradation in a manner that distinguished clearly between the national interests and historical legacies of industrialised and developing countries, Indira Gandhi's speech argued that, for developing nations, socio-economic development must come before environmental protection: 'the environmental problems of developing countries are not the side effects of excessive industrialization', she noted, 'but reflect the inadequacy of development'.[57] In a formulation that would be cited into the future, she argued,

> We do not wish to impoverish the environment any further and yet we cannot for a moment forget the grim poverty of large numbers of people. Are not poverty and need the greatest polluters?[58]

Indira Gandhi's interventions at Stockholm highlighted how international environmental policy-making was linked to 'a range of broader concerns associated with poverty and equity and the nature of the global political economy'.[59] Crucially, she also underscored a historical dimension to environmental degradation, arguing that 'many of the advanced countries of today have reached their present affluence by their domination over other races and countries, the exploitation of their own masses and their own natural resources'.[60] She insisted that industrialised countries rectify both their damage to the environment and the impediments to development and prosperity they had imposed upon former colonies. Indira Gandhi's defensive, principled and development-prioritising stance drew a standing ovation,[61] won generous media coverage, and according to one observer, 'eloquently expressed the position of the Third World countries'.[62] The differences in position revealed the same tensions inherent in the relations between the industrialised OECD countries of the North, and the poorer, developing G77 countries of the South that animated calls for an NIEO. In debating ways to mitigate global environmental degradation, the conference brought to the fore conflicting ideas on sovereignty, sustainable development and the appropriate generation and distribution of funding to bring about change. These issues would for decades feature at the heart of debates over international cooperation over the mitigation of environmental degradation.

A fourth significant counter-order moment for India came in the wake of the sixth Non-Aligned summit, convened in Havana in 1979 under the chairmanship of Cuba. Cuba's aim at the Summit was to accelerate what one contemporary observer described as the Non-Aligned Movement's 'leftward shift',[63] specifically, to entrench within the Movement the long-held Cuban conviction that the Soviet Camp constituted a 'natural ally' of the Non-Aligned nations.[64] While Cuba was less effective at 'radicalising' the Movement at Havana than critics had anticipated, the Summit's final declararion contained more criticism of the West than had any other summit declararion.[65] In the wake of the Sixth Summit, concerns and accusations circulated within the international media and among governments that the NAM had 'lost its claim to being non-aligned' by swinging toward the Soviet Union.[66]

Any support that Cuban chairmanship gained at Havana for the argument that the Soviet Union was a natural NAM ally was rapidly undone by the movement of Soviet troops into Afghanistan – a NAM member – in late 1979. A majority of Non-Aligned nations condemned the Soviet invasion on two separate occasions within the UN General Assembly in the course of 1980.[67] It was in this context that, in

February 1981, India offered to host the Foreign Ministers' Conference of the Non-Aligned Countries – a meeting held between summits – some months earlier than originally planned. P. V. Narasimha Rao, then minister of external affairs, sent out an invitation to the Conference in which he underscored the necessity of 'reassert[ing] the image of the movement as an independent, moral, and political force in international relations, and as a positive factor of peace and security'.[68]

While some Non-Aligned states were sceptical owing to India's own alleged tilt toward the Soviet Union, given the Indo–Soviet Treaty of Friendship signed in 1971, the conference offered India the opportunity to demonstrate neutrality and seek a consensus among NAM members. The New Delhi Declaration that issued from the Conference 'was evenly balanced between the two Cold War blocs' in that it expressed criticism of the United States only once, and presented – for the first time in the history of the Non-Aligned Movement – indirect criticism of two socialist states (the Soviet Union owing to the Afghan invasion, and Vietnam due to its invasion of Kampuchea in 1978).[69]

One Indian commentator claimed that the New Delhi Foreign Ministers' Conference was a 'landmark in the history of the movement of the non-aligned states' that 'to many observers symbolized a return to the original principles and genuine non-alignment of the founding fathers of the movement'.[70] Indeed, the conference 'undoubtedly... served the main objective of the majority of members ... namely of pulling it back to a more balanced and "equidistant" position between the two Cold War blocs'.[71] In the wake of the Foreign Ministers' Conference came the Seventh Non-Aligned Summit in 1983. This was also convened in Delhi, having been diverted from the originally intended venue of Baghdad owing to the ongoing war between Iraq and Iran.[72] The Seventh Summit drew together more Non-Aligned heads of state and government than any previous summit, testifying to the faith members had in India's chairmanship.[73] K. Natwar Singh, secretary in the ministry of external affairs from 1982 to 1984, served as the secretary-general to the Seventh Summit, which, he reported, 'turned out to be the least controversial and most constructive of all Non-Aligned Summits'.[74]

Yet, even as Indian foreign policy continued with Nehru's stress on global leadership through alternative means to the power politics of the Cold War, India's strategic behaviour in its own neighbourhood took a more conventional turn. The 1970s and 1980s witnessed a series of military interventions designed to preserve the regional order in line with Indian security interests. Certainly, efforts to project strategic restraint and moral justification accompanied Indian policy in the region. Indian officials sought to present the 1971 war with Pakistan that resulted in the formation of Bangladesh as an intervention on humanitarian grounds, although this framing was not accepted by the UN Security Council.[75] India intervened briefly and successfully in East Pakistan but withdrew its forces almost immediately once liberation was complete and promptly returned territory seized from Pakistan in the West. In a letter to Richard Nixon, Indira Gandhi explained that '[we] sought nothing for ourselves, neither territory nor special privileges, only everlasting peace'.[76] This claim was not entirely credible. Few disagree that, while the massacres occurring in East Pakistan and the enormous flow of refugees into India were important factors, a divided Pakistan was also a strategically sound outcome for India, since it weakened a long-term antagonist. Yet attempts to project a moral case for the decision to intervene, which was not empty rhetoric since it was backed up with evidence of self-restraint after the conclusion of the war, were important signals that India's foreign policy was still guided by moral imperatives.

Indira Gandhi's 1972 article in *Foreign Affairs* sought to provide further reassurance that her government had no intention of transforming India into a 'typical power' and that a basic continuity lay at the root of Indian foreign policy:

> India's foreign policy is a projection of the values which we have cherished through the centuries as well as our current concern. We are not tied to the traditional concepts of a foreign policy designed to safeguard overseas possessions, investments, the carving out of spheres of influence and the erection of *cordons sanitaires* ... Our first concern has been to prevent any erosion of our independence ... Non-alignment ... implied neither non-involvement nor neutrality. It was and is an assertion of our freedom of judgement and action.[77]

Such reassurances appeared hollow from a regional perspective, however. Indira Gandhi's attempts to maintain peace and stability in South Asia and protect India from great power interference in the region, while defensive in intent, could not but intimidate India's neighbours. With a substantial import of Soviet arms, India built up a rising military profile and generated considerable insecurity among them.

The Indian victory in the 1971 war consolidated India's power and prestige over the whole of the Subcontinent. India's longstanding resistance to external interference in the Indo–Pakistan dispute eventually extended to the rest of South Asia and further to the Indian Ocean region. Under Indira Gandhi's leadership and beyond, India reserved the right to be the only legitimate state to intervene in the region.

At the same time, India's expanding military capability brought with it the confidence to assume the role of 'regional security manager' in the Subcontinent.[78] This was not an entirely self-appointed function. Indeed, since India's emulation of the major powers did not affect their direct interests, neither the United States nor the Soviet Union had any apprehensions about its newly assumed role. Under the leadership of Rajiv Gandhi – Indira Gandhi's son and successor – from 1984 to 1989, the United States acquiesced to India's military interventions in Sri Lanka and the Maldives, legitimising India's role as a regional policeman.[79] 'Operation Cactus', as India's 1988 intervention in the Maldives was known, has been described by one contemporary analyst as 'a model for the benign security role that India could play in the Indian Ocean'.[80] After rescuing Maldivian president Abdul Gayoom from an attempted coup, India drew praise from both US president Ronald Reagan and British prime minister Margaret Thatcher.[81] Indian cabinet secretary B. G. Deshmukh claimed that the operation 'enhanced India's prestige enormously'.[82]

The Sri Lankan involvement, however, ended in disaster when a military intervention, ostensibly agreed to by the Sri Lankan government but in effect carried out under duress, degenerated into a violent and effective counterinsurgency operation eventually abetted by the Sri Lankan government, and Indian troops were withdrawn in 1990.[83] India's emerging status as a regional power drew calls from Nepal for a 'zone of peace' in South Asia, from Bangladesh for the designation of the Bay of Bengal as a 'Pocket of Peace', and from the Maldives for the United Nations to develop a special mechanism for the security of small states.[84] Security concerns were also expressed in Australia, Indonesia and Malaysia.[85] In the region, India was gaining status, not for the moral leadership that its leaders still claimed to be seeking, but on account of the application of its growing military capacity.

On the whole, while India's counter-order position earned it considerable respect, it is arguable that its emergence as a regional power with the military muscle to shape the strategic landscape did so just as much. Thus, India simultaneously opposed the international norm of power politics in the global setting while embracing and applying it at the regional level. This twin strategy brought it status in different ways that as yet did not find themselves significantly in contradiction.

Non-proliferation

Just as India sought to challenge the division of the world into two warring blocs through its efforts to establish and secure the autonomy of the NAM, so in the post-Nehru era India sought to resist the consolidation of a bifurcated nuclear order, divided materially and socially between powers who were permitted to possess nuclear weapons, and those who were not.

In 1965, Sisir Gupta, a diplomat and academic, had referred to India as the 'sixth Power in a world where only five are recognized to be great'.[86] He saw that India could 'either enter the club by defying the world and making a bomb or see to it that the bomb as a status symbol loses its significance because of effective progress towards disarmament'.[87] At the time Gupta was writing, an Indian delegate at the conference of the Eighteen Nation Disarmament Committee (ENDC), which ran from 1962 to 1968, was attempting precisely this latter strategy. V. C. Trivedi, who joined the negotiations as the Indian representative from 1964 onwards, spoke at length within the conference about the problematic nature of the prestige that had become attached to nuclear weapons, arguing in 1966 that 'there should be no enshrinement or perpetuation of a privileged status of nuclear Powers'.[88]

It became clear, however, that no headway could be made towards universal disarmament of the kind Trivedi sought on behalf of India. By early 1967, the Soviet Union and the United States had developed the joint draft of a treaty on nuclear non-proliferation, endorsed by the United Kingdom.[89] Chandra Shekhar Jha, foreign secretary from February 1965 to August 1967, recalled how 'implicit in the draft treaty was the recognition by the rest of the world of the legitimacy of the possession and use by the five countries (USA, USSR, UK, China and France) which already possessed them'.[90] M. C. Chagla, who served as India's minister for external affairs in 1966–67, noted how

> we had strong objections to the treaty on the grounds, first, that it created a nuclear monopoly; secondly, that it discriminated between nuclear and non-nuclear powers; thirdly, that it prevented the underdeveloped countries from acquiring nuclear knowledge which they could use for technological advance.[91]

Despite limited alterations to the drafts of the treaty, this position was to remain the official Indian stance.

The 1968 Non-Proliferation Treaty, which came into force in 1970, consolidated a global nuclear order with a distinct hierarchy in which Nuclear-Weapons States stood above Non-Nuclear Weapon States, with only the former regarded as the legitimate bearers of nuclear arms. In addition, the regime brought about a shift in global nuclear norms: whereas nuclear testing was considered 'prestigious and legitimate' in the 1960s, any country testing or acquiring nuclear capabilities after 1 January 1967 was deemed to be 'illegitimate and irresponsible'.[92]

India's 'Peaceful Nuclear Explosion' conducted at Pokhran in May 1974 was in some ways India's answer to the NPT. In the wake of the explosion, Indira Gandhi insisted that nuclear energy would continue to be used only for peaceful purposes and that India had no intention of making a nuclear bomb. In a parliamentary address on 22 July 1974, echoing Trivedi's earlier statements at the ENCD, she emphasised that '[n]o technology is evil in itself. It is the use that nations make of technology which determines its character. India does not accept the principle of apartheid in any matter and technology is no exception'.[93] The test was a message of defiance, but a display of capacity rather than aggression. While the notion of a 'peaceful explosion' bemused onlookers, it was fully in line with the technological aspirations of the elite, reassured those lobbying for a nuclear deterrent, and did not disavow India's peaceful approach. The identity projected was that of a nuclear power, not a nuclear weapons power. Through the test, India, according to one Indian commentator, became 'the only country that has voluntarily restricted itself to purely peaceful explosions of atomic devices – a uniqueness which some countries still look at with suspicion'.[94]

Ashis Nandy, shortly after the 1974 explosion, attempted to provide 'some idea of the psychopolitical environment within which India may have decided to go nuclear'. His findings were that the vast majority of the eighty elites[95] he interviewed were both against India's acquisition of nuclear weapons and viewed the NPT negatively. According to Nandy, '[t]he most frequent reasons given for the rejection of the NPT were that the treaty was "dishonest and unequal" ... and that it did not curb the nuclear powers and was designed to preserve the nuclear status quo'.[96] He surmised that '[t]he responses are obviously interrelated in that they both articulated the theme of an in-group, from which second class nations like India were excluded'.[97] An editorial in the *Economic and Political Weekly*, too, saw in the Treaty an attempt by the 'nuclear Brahmins' to acquire a perpetual place at the top of a 'well-defined status hierarchy'.[98] To sign the Treaty would be an act of collaboration in India's international diminishment.

At the same time, however, the 'Peaceful Nuclear Explosion' of 1974 pushed India out of the recently consolidated international norms on proliferation issues, which was to have even more serious implications for Indian aspirations to occupy an influential role in global affairs. If, in not signing the NPT, India had hoped to avoid nuclear apartheid, through the 1974 nuclear test, India was served with its own tailor-made version. The 1974 nuclear explosion was met with punitive responses that were to endure for at least three decades, and many of these were designed specifically with India in mind. The United States and Canada ceased all nuclear cooperation with India, and the US Congress passed a series of legislative curbs[99] in the 1970s that restricted military and economic assistance to countries receiving nuclear weapons-related equipment, materials or technology in the absence of full-scope International Atomic Energy Agency safeguards.[100] Limitations that began in the mid-1970s continued into the 1980s and 1990s, particularly with the establishment and the growth of multilateral technology denial regimes, such as the 1987 Missile Technology Control Regime, which attempted to slow down transfer of dual-use materials and technology, and the 1974 Nuclear Suppliers Group, which attempted to control it. The net of sanctions that denied India access to nuclear material, technology and equipment was extensive and stultifying. It was also unsustainable. India's de facto isolation and vulnerability on nuclear issues would finally came to a head within the context of the negotiations over the Comprehensive Test Ban Treaty negotiations in the mid-1990s.

Importantly, however, having not signed the NPT, India's delegates could continue their principled articulation of an alternative vision of global nuclear disarmament, based on universal and non-discriminatory principles, both at UN fora and within the standing Geneva Conference on Disarmament. A rejection of the NPT certainly enabled India to retain its nuclear option. But perhaps more importantly, it permitted the Nehruvian vision to live on.

Strong postures on issues pertaining to disarmament thus continued. A comprehensive ban on nuclear weapons testing was proposed, together with other disarmament measurements, by Morarji Desai at a special session of the UN General Assembly on 9 June 1978.[101] Exactly a decade later to the day, Rajiv Gandhi unveiled his Action Plan on Nuclear Disarmament at the special UN Session on Disarmament in 1988.[102] At the centre of this plan were proposals for a comprehensive test ban and global cut-off in fissile materials production, together with a proposal for a deal that tied India and other potential nuclear weapons states to forgoing nuclear weapons if the existing nuclear powers agreed to phase out their own weapons stockpile by 2010, beginning with a 50 per cent reduction in US and Soviet arsenals.[103] This strategy suggested that India considered itself to possess bargaining power even from outside the NPT, but the initiative was rejected by the United States.

India's assertion of an independent position on nuclear weapons on balance probably did not add much to its status, though its self-image remained positive. Testing a single nuclear weapon but not building an arsenal brought no significant outside support, and even less capacity, for pushing its disarmament agenda. On the contrary, India became something of a renegade from the standpoint of the major power norm of non-proliferation and was to feel increasing pressure. Ironically, as we show in the next chapter, a stronger challenge to the non-proliferation norm in 1998 – combined with other factors – brought greater strategic, and arguably status, returns.

Democracy and the liberal economic order

During the post-Nehru era, India struggled to retain its status as the world's largest democracy, but was able to survive significant challenges. The foremost was a period of emergency rule under Indira Gandhi in the mid-1970s and the subsequent fragmentation of its 'one-party-dominant' political system that led to an era of unstable coalitions.

In 1975, Indira Gandhi was convicted under Indian law of 'corrupt electoral practices' dating back to the 1971 elections, and was banned from voting or participating in parliamentary proceedings. With opposition parties and some portions of the media calling for her resignation, she imposed a national emergency for 21 months, suspending the constitution, imprisoning thousands of political opponents, and imposing rigid press censorship.[104] The official US response to Indira Gandhi's period of emergency rule was muted,[105] although the US media was less forgiving: in July, *Time* magazine labelled Indira Gandhi 'imperious', her leadership as 'near dictatorial', and characterised India as 'struggling through a political crisis that would profoundly affect [its] future'.[106] Opting to hold general elections in March 1977, Indira suffered a decisive electoral defeat, an outcome that appeared to provide confirmation to 'Western proponents of liberal democracy' of India's democratic model.[107] Yet Indira Gandhi was subsequently re-elected in January 1980 when the opposition Janata Party, which had taken office in 1977 under the premiership of Morarji Desai, collapsed due to infighting, and subsequently Charan Singh, the leader of the breakaway faction and brief successor party, the Lok Dal, lost a no-confidence vote.[108] Indira Gandhi had triumphed despite the authoritarian interlude, and while it was not immediately clear to outsiders what this heralded for India's future, regular elections continued and there was no return to emergency rule. In the longer term, as the episode receded into history, it came to be seen as an unfortunate aberration in India's democratic experience. Post-Cold War India was to derive much mileage from its demonstrated political resilience as a democracy.

As far as India's economic odyssey was concerned, the effort to achieve status through the creative strategy of building an alternative world economic system and challenging the world economic order that centred on the major capitalist powers and their interests was singularly unsuccessful. India had not managed to transform the world economy before integrating with it. The debt crisis of the 1980s at one extreme, and the phenomenal economic successes of Taiwan, Singapore and South Korea – who sought development through exports rather than self-reliance – at the other, rendered impossible any common Global South economic consensus, with the bloc left 'palpably weaker, more differentiated, and less unified'.[109] An emphasis on liberal trading regimes began to spread among much of the South, including within India.[110] From the mid-1970s India's leaders sought to liberalise economic policy, though even this was politically challenging, given the manner in which popular pressures and the exigencies of electoral politics impeded major policy departures.[111] By 1989, one critical Indian observer delivered the following damning verdict on India's Global South solidarity:

> Far from being involved in the strivings of and acting in solidarity with G-77 and the non-aligned movement, India is now ready to work … directly for accommodation within the wider framework of a world order as ordained by the wider economic, political and strategic interests of the G-7.[112]

The upshot was that India's status remained low as an economic player in a world that was changing rapidly. It required, as we will see in the next chapter, an economic shock to dislodge India decisively from its self-imposed self-sufficiency rut.

Conclusion

In the post-Nehru era, India followed the path of the great powers in seeking to acquire military power and, to a significant extent, matched great power strategic behaviour in its immediate neighbourhood. India also came to depend on the Soviet Union to back it strategically at a time when it felt threatened with isolation, which was the discomfiting result of a continued strategy of seeking to maintain a distance from the big powers. Strong continuities were visible in India's enduring preference for economic self-sufficiency, tailing off only in the late 1970s and 1980s as India took gradual steps to liberalise. However, even as India rejected global capitalism in its prevailing form, it was forced to lean heavily on the system's economic centre, the United States, first for succour in the form of food aid and subsequently for assistance in revolutionising agricultural production.

At the same time, India's attempts to innovate normatively by challenging dominant political and economic structures continued. This was reflected in the prominent role it sought within the evolution and development of the NAM, in early environmental activism, and in its contributions to the establishment and activism of the Group of 77. India also challenged the material and social bifurcation of the nuclear order that came to be embodied in the NPT, at first by not signing the Treaty. The challenge then went further, as Indira Gandhi sanctioned the conducting of a nuclear test, ultimately carving out an innovative status for India as a nuclear-capable power but not a nuclear-armed power. This enabled India to break out from a lower-status position as a non-nuclear state, even while it damaged Indian status, since India was, at least in part, in contravention of dominant non-proliferation norms. The decision not to immediately weaponise India's nuclear programme also permitted India, nominally at least, to maintain a pro-disarmament stance, but conceivably relegated it to low status as an outsider going against dominant non-proliferation norms.

The overall pattern that emerges in the post-Nehru era is a partial Indian shift in relation to the dominant associational sources of status through the acquisition of conventional but not nuclear arms, and through expedient proximity to major powers when required. This was accompanied by a continuation of its previous rejection of dominant norms through a range of counter-order efforts at the global level, but adoption of similar strategic behaviour in its immediate environs.

Notes

1   Norris, Robert S. and Hans M. Kristensen, 'Global Nuclear Inventories, 1945–2013', *Bulletin of the Atomic Scientists*, vol. 69, no. 5 (2013), p. 78, figure 2.
2   Kennedy, Paul,*The Rise and Fall of the Great Powers: Economic Change and Military Conflict from 1500 to 2000* (New York: Random House, 1987), pp. 525–535; Bellon, Bertrand and George Niosi, *The Decline of the American Economy*, trans. Robert Chodos and Ellen Garmaise (Montreal and New York: Black Rose Books, 1989), esp. pp. 9–65.
3   Cooper, Richard, 'Economic Interdependence and Foreign Policy in the Seventies', *World Politics*, vol. 24, no. 2 (January 1972), pp. 159–181; Rosenau, James N., *The Study of Global Interdependence: Essays on the Transnationalization of World Affairs* (London: Frances Pinter, 1980).
4   Munro, Ross H., 'Superpower Rising', *Time* (3 April 1989), pp. 6–13.

5 Krishna, Gopal, 'India and the International Order: Retreat from Idealism', in Hedley Bull and Adam Watson, eds, *The Expansion of International Society* (Oxford: Clarendon Press, 1984), pp. 269–288.

6 Gandhi, Indira, 'Preface', in Planning Commission, *4th Five-Year Plan* (New Delhi: Government of India, 1970), available at: http://planning commission.nic.in/plans/planrel/fiveyr/4th/4ppre.htm (accessed on 2 December 2016).

7 Harrison, Selig, *India: The Most Dangerous Decades* (Princeton, NJ: Princeton University Press, 1960), p. 319.

8 Hardgrave, Robert L. and Stanley A. Kochanek, *India: Government and Politics in a Developing Nation (Sixth Edition)* (Orlando, FL: Harcourt, Brace & Co., 2000) p. 259.

9 World Bank, 'World Bank National Accounts Data'.

10 Ganguly, Sumit and Rahul Mukherji, *India since 1980* (Cambridge: Cambridge University Press, 2011), p. 60. The term 'Hindu rate of growth' was coined by economist Raj Krishna and does not, oddly enough, carry religious connotations.

11 Ganguly and Mukherji, *India since 1980*, p. 60; McCartney, Matthew, *India the Political Economy of Growth, Stagnation, and the State, 1951–2007* (Abingdon and New York: Routledge, 2009), pp. 151–178.

12 World Bank, 'World Bank National Accounts Data'.

13 Chari, P. R., 'Indo-Soviet Military Cooperation: A Review', *Asian Survey*, vol. XIX, no. 3, March 1979, p. 236.

14 Stockholm International Peace Research Institute, Military Expenditure Database, www.sipri.org/databases/milex (accessed on 26 November 2016).

15 Stockholm International Peace Research Institute, 'SIPRI Military Expenditure Database'.

16 Ibid.

17 Wolf, Charles, et al., *Long-Term Economic and Military Trends, 1950–2010*, Santa Monica, CA: RAND, April 1989, p. 23, table 7. The dollar amounts are in constant 1986 dollars.

18 Wolf et al., *Long-Term Economic and Military Trends*, p. 17, table 5. The compared amounts are in 1986 dollars.

19 Copley, Gregory, 'Inevitable India, Inevitable Power', *Defense and Foreign Affairs*, vol. XVI, no.12 (December 1988), pp. 29 and 52.

20 Lall, Arthur Samuel, *The Emergence of Modern India* (New York: Columbia University Press, 1981), p. 138.

21 Gupta, Sisir, *India and the International System* (New Delhi: Vikas, 1981), p. 243.

22 Bajpai, G. S., 'India and the Balance of Power', *Indian Yearbook of International Affairs*, vol. 1 (1952), pp. 1–8.

23 Mansingh, Surjit, *India's Search for Power* (New Delhi: Sage, 1984), p. 2.

24 Indira Gandhi, cited in: Tharoor, Shashi, *Reasons of State: Political Development and India's Foreign Policy Under Indira Gandhi, 1966–1977* (New Delhi: Vikas, 1982), p. 88.

25 Basrur, Rajesh M., *Minimum Deterrence and India's Nuclear Security* (Stanford, CA: Stanford University Press, 2006), pp. 59–67.

26 Subrahmanyam, K., 'Indian Nuclear Policy, 1964–98 (A Personal Recollection)', in Jasjit Singh, ed., *Nuclear India* (New Delhi: Knowledge World, 1998), p. 27.

27   Brands, H. W., *India and the United States: The Cold Peace* (Boston: Twayne Publishers, 1990), p. 137.
28   Chagla, M. C., *Roses in December: An Autobiography* (Bombay: Bharatiya Vidya Bhavan, 1974), p. 424.
29   Goertz Lall, Betty, 'Notes from Asia and Germany', *Bulletin of the Atomic Scientists* (November 1965), p. 33; Nandy, Ashis, 'Between Two Gandhis: Psychopolitical Aspects of the Nuclearization of India', *Asian Survey*, vol. 14, no. 11 (November 1974), pp. 966–970.
30   Chengappa, Raj, *Weapons of Peace* (New Delhi: HarperCollins, 2000), p. 260.
31   Chengappa, *Weapons of Peace*, p. 304.
32   World Bank, 'World Bank National Accounts Data, and OECD National Accounts Data Files', http://data.worldbank.org/indicator/NE.TRD. GNFS.ZS?end=1990&start=1964 (accessed on 26 November 2016).
33   Merrill, Dennis, *Bread and the Ballot* (Chapel Hill: University of North Carolina Press, 1990), p. 1.
34   Nayar, Baldev Raj and T. V. Paul, *India in the World Order: Searching for Major Power Status* (Cambridge: Cambridge University Press, 2003), p. 169.
35   Mansingh, *India's Search for Power*, pp. 316–381.
36   Parayil, Govindan, 'The Green Revolution in India: A Case Study of Technological Change', *Technology and Culture*, vol. 33, no. 4 (1992), pp. 737–756.
37   Gandhi, Indira, 'Preface', in Planning Commission, *4th Five-Year Plan* (New Delhi: Government of India, 1970).
38   Ibid.
39   Calculated from World Bank, 'World Bank National Accounts Data, and OECD National Accounts Data Files', http://data.worldbank.org/indicator/ NY.GDP.MKTP.CD?end=1990&start=1964 (accessed on 26 November 2016).
40   'Text of the Indo-Soviet Treaty', *Mainstream*, 13 August 2011, www.ma instreamweekly.net/article2950.html (accessed on 27 November 2016).
41   Keenleyside, T. A., 'Prelude to Power: The Meaning of Non-Alignment before Indian Independence', *Pacific Affairs*, vol. 53, no. 3 (1980), p. 463.
42   Willetts, Peter, *The Non-Aligned Movement: The Origins of a Third World Alliance* (London: Frances Pinter, 1978), p. 12.
43   Jha, Chandra Shekhar, *From Bandung to Tashkent: Glimpses of India's Foreign Policy* (Delhi: Sangam Books, 1983), p. 252.
44   Ibid.
45   Ibid., p. 253.
46   Abraham, Itty, 'From Bandung to NAM: Non-alignment and Indian Foreign Policy, 1947–65', *Commonwealth and Comparative Politics*, vol. 46, no. 2 (2008), pp. 195–219; Willetts, *The Non-Aligned Movement*; Rubinoff, Arthur G. 'The Multilateral Imperative in India's Foreign Policy', *The Round Table*, no. 319 (1991), pp. 313–334.
47   Jha, *From Bandung to Tashkent*, p. 253.
48   Ibid., p. 266.
49   Abraham, 'From Bandung to NAM', p. 215.
50   Abraham, 'From Bandung to NAM', p. 196; Nesadurai, Helen E.S. 'Bandung and the Political Economy of North–South Relations: Sowing the Seeds for Re-visioning International Society', in See Seng Tan

and Amitav Acharya, eds, *Bandung Revisited: The Legacy of the Asian-African Conference for International Order* (Singapore: NUS Press, 2008), p. 77.

51 Sen, Sunanda, 'New International Economic Order and Contemporary World Economic Scene', *Economic and Political Weekly*, vol. 16, no. 10/12 (March 1981), pp. 516–525; Harshe, Rajen, 'India's Nonalignment: An Attempt at Conceptual Reconstruction', *Economic and Political Weekly* (17–24 February 1990), p. 403.

52 Mansingh, *India's Search for Power*, pp. 361–387.

53 Ibid., p. 325.

54 Kochanek, S. A., 'India's Changing Role in the United Nations', *Pacific Affairs*, vol. 53, no. 1 (1980), p. 56.

55 'BM', 'Toeing the G-7 Line', *Economic and Political Weekly* (18 February 1989), p. 344.

56 Elliott, Lorraine, *The Global Politics of the Environment*. 2nd edn (New York: New York University Press, 2004), p. 7.

57 Gandhi, Indira, 'Address of Shrimati Indira Gandhi, Prime Minister of India: The Unfinished Revolution', Part V of 'A Special Report: What Happened at Stockholm', *Bulletin of the Atomic Scientists*, vol. XXVIII, no. 7 (September 1972), p. 37.

58 Gandhi, 'Address of Shrimati Indira Gandhi', p. 36.

59 Elliott, *The Global Politics of the Environment*, p. 24.

60 Gandhi, 'Address of Shrimati Indira Gandhi', p. 36.

61 Jacobsen, Sally 'A Call to Environmental Order', Part II of 'A Special Report: What Happened at Stockholm', *Bulletin of the Atomic Scientists*, vol. XXVIII, no. 7 (September 1972), p. 24.

62 Rajan, Mukund Govind, *Global Environmental Politics: India and the North–South Politics of Global Environmental Issues* (Delhi: Oxford University Press, 1997), p. 27.

63 LeoGrande, William M., 'Evolution of the Nonaligned Movement', *Problems of Communism* (January–February 1980), p. 50.

64 LeoGrande, 'Evolution of the Nonaligned Movement'.

65 Ibid., pp. 40–50.

66 Rajan, M. S., 'The Non-Aligned Movement: The New Delhi Conference and After', *Southeast Asian Affairs* (1 January 1982), p. 60.

67 Ibid.

68 Ibid., p. 70.

69 Ibid., p. 68.

70 Ibid., p. 71.

71 Ibid., p. 67.

72 Singham, A. W. and Shirley Hune, *Non-alignment in an Age of Alignments* (London: Zed), p. 245.

73 Singh, K. Natwar, 'The Seventh Non-Aligned Summit, New Delhi, March 1983', *The Round Table*, no. 287 (1983), pp. 328–330.

74 Ibid., p. 328.

75 Wheeler, Nicholas J., *Saving Strangers: Humanitarian Intervention in International Society* (Oxford: Oxford University Press, 2000).

76 Indira Gandhi, cited in: Mansingh, *India's Search for Power*, p. 38.

77 Gandhi, Indira, 'India's Foreign Policy', *Foreign Affairs*, vol. 51, no. 65 (1972), pp. 65–77.

78   Marshall M. Bouton, cited in: Basrur, Rajesh M., *India's External Relations: A Theoretical Analysis* (New Delhi: Commonwealth Publishers, 2000), p. 95.
79   Chopra, Pran, 'India: Regional Supercop?' *Express Magazine* (21 May 1989), p. I.
80   Brewster, David, *India's Ocean: The Story of India's Bid for Regional Leadership* (Abingdon: Routledge, 2014), p. 58.
81   Ibid.
82   B. G. Deshmukh, cited in: Brewster, *India's Ocean*, p. 58.
83   Brewster, *India's Ocean*, p. 50–52.
84   Basrur, Rajesh, 'India: A Major Power in the Making', in Thomas J. Volgy, Renato Corbetta, Keith A. Grant and Ryan G. Baird, eds, *Major Powers and the Quest for Status in International Politics: Global and Regional Perspectives* (New York: Palgrave, 2011), p. 187.
85   Basrur, Rajesh M., *India's External Relations: A Theoretical Analysis* (New Delhi: Commonwealth Publishers, 2000), p. 90; Datta-Ray, Sunanda K., 'Region's New Bogey?', *Statesman* (5 March 1989), reprinted in *Indian Ocean Review*, vol. 2, no. 2 (June 1989), p. I.
86   Gupta, *India and the International System*, p. 243.
87   Ibid.
88   Trivedi, cited in: Sullivan, Kate, 'The Evolution of India's Great Power Identity: A Powerful Performance', Ph.D. Dissertation, Australian National University, April 2011, p. 203.
89   Jha, *From Bandung to Tashkent*, p. 299.
90   Ibid., p. 300.
91   Chagla, *Roses in December*, p. 424.
92   Sagan, Scott D., 'Why Do States Build Nuclear Weapons? Three Models in Search of a Bomb', *International Security*, vol. 21, no. 3 (1996–1997), p. 76.
93   Indira Gandhi, cited in: Rajan, M. S., 'India: A Case of Power without Force', *International Journal*, vol. 30, no. 2 (1995), p. 303.
94   Lall, *The Emergence of Modern India*, p. 182.
95   According to Nandy, these elites 'may have had some direct or indirect voice in the decision-making processes of the Indian polity' and constituted a 'fair cross-section of the accessible universe of decision-makers at the time'. Nandy, Ashis, 'Between Two Gandhis: Psychopolitical Aspects of the Nuclearization of India', *Asian Survey*, vol. 14, no. 11 (November 1974), pp. 966–967.
96   Ibid.
97   Ibid.
98   'Non-Proliferation Humbug', *Economic and Political Weekly*, vol. 3, no. 11 (16 March 1968), p. 441.
99   These included the Symington amendment to the Foreign Aid Bill of 1976 and the Nuclear Nonproliferation Act of 1978.
100   Ganguly, Sumit, 'India's Pathway to Pokhran II: The Prospects and Sources of New Delhi's Nuclear Weapons Program', *International Security*, vol. 23, no. 4 (1999), p. 161; Chellaney, Brahma, *Nuclear Proliferation: The U.S.–Indian Conflict* (New Delhi: Orient Longman, 1993).
101   Ghose, Arundhati, 'Negotiating the CTBT: India's Security Concerns and Nuclear Disarmament', *Journal of International Affairs*, vol. 51, no. 1 (1997), p. 243.

102 Frankel, Francine R., 'Preface', in Francine R. Frankel, ed., *Bridging the Non-Proliferation Divide: The United States and India* (Delhi: Konark, 1995), p. vi.
103 Harrison, Selig S., 'The Forgotten Bargain', *World Policy Journal* (Fall 2006), p. 3.
104 Hardgrave and Kochanek, *India: Government and Politics*, pp. 260–261.
105 Ray, Jayanta Kumar, *India's Foreign Relations, 1947–2007* (New Delhi: Routledge, 2011), ch. 10.
106 'India: Indira Gandhi's Dictatorship Digs In', *Time Magazine*, 14 July 1975, available at http://content.time.com/time/magazine/article/0,9171, 917627,00.html (accessed 28 November 2016).
107 Klieman, Aaron S., 'Indira's India: Democracy and Crisis Government', *Political Science Quarterly*, vol. 96, no. 2 (Summer, 1981), p. 242.
108 Gupte, Pranay, *Mother India: A Political Biography of Indira Gandhi* (New York: Macmillan, 1992), p. 110.
109 Ravenhill, John, 'The North–South Balance of Power', *International Affairs*, vol. 6, no. 4 (1990), p. 731.
110 Alden, Chris, Sally Morphet and Marco Antonio Vieira, *The Non-Aligned Movement and Group of 77 During the Cold War, 1965–89* (Basingstoke: Palgrave Macmillan), p. 58.
111 Kohli, Atul, 'Politics of Economic Liberalization in India', *World Development*, vol. 17, no. 3 (1989), pp. 305–328.
112 'BM', 'Toeing the G-7 Line'.

4 Status and power in the post-Cold War era (1991–2016)

Introduction

This chapter explores India's attempts at seeking status during the post-Cold War period from 1991 onwards. India's relationship with the dominant normative order underwent a significant shift in the post-Cold War era. During the preceding period, despite a new interest in the acquisition of military power, India had retained much of its older character, notably a continued resistance to association with the great powers and global capitalism. Broadly speaking, from 1991 onwards, India sought to embrace the system and simultaneously to seek higher status within it, placing emphasis on normative conformity rather than 'counter-order' innovation. In essence, India's status-seeking strategy underwent what might be called a Kuhnian 'revolution' in the early 1990s. Previously, Indian policy makers had viewed India as a weak state subject to the unwelcome pressures of great power politics, and had sought to keep these pressures at bay. As a result, Indian efforts centred on locating political and economic relationships as far as possible outside the dominant power structures of the time. From the 1990s, India shifted direction and sought to conform to much – though not all – of the dominant normative order. It embarked on a process of integration with the dominant political and economic structures of the global system. Buoyed by a new confidence generated by accelerated economic growth and rising military prowess, Indian leaders moved decisively to seek higher status as a future great power.

The fresh quest for status: drivers

A number of profound changes in the global strategic landscape propelled India's turn to a more conformist status-seeking strategy in the post-Cold War era.[1] First, a major balance of payments problem, building up after 1985, had produced a severe economic crisis by 1990. India had to seek succour from the International Monetary Fund (IMF), which expectedly called for 'structural adjustment' by way of liberal reforms as a precondition for rescue. It is worth noting that the IMF's loan was made available only after India physically transferred 47 tonnes of gold to the Bank of England in the summer of 1991 as collateral – an experience that led to a widespread outcry and lamentations over India's humiliation.[2] Indian status had hit a new low. But the experience also provided the trigger for rethinking policy. As Finance Minister Manmohan Singh put it in Parliament, 'all of us in this House and our people outside must reflect as to what has gone wrong with this country that we have to do such painful things'.[3] Galvanised by the shock, the government under P. V. Narasimha Rao, prime minister from 1991 to 1996, began dismantling the extensive controls that had long hobbled the Indian economy and set in motion an era of speedier growth. This in turn gave rise to a new sense of self-assurance that reawakened the desire for higher status. India's emerging image as a country with a dynamic economy also stirred interest among the major powers, who, after the turn of the millennium, began to view India as an 'emerging market' and a potential major player in the world economy.[4]

Second, the Cold War wound down rapidly after 1989, altering the strategic landscape and forcing India to rethink its strategic foundations. The Non-Aligned Movement (NAM), crafted as an alternative to the dominance of Cold War politics, faced an existential challenge: there was nothing vis-à-vis which India and other member states could now be non-aligned. The dissolution of the Soviet Union also took away India's main pillar of support on key aspects of its security: assured supply of advanced weapons, oblique containment of China, and political backing on the sensitive issue of Kashmir. India, conscious too of the need for foreign investment and technology, responded by turning to the United States, which – after a brief interregnum during which it had seemed to be coming to terms with Beijing – was also looking for a partner to contain China.

Third, India's shift from covert to overt nuclear weapons capability was decisive in changing its position in the international system. After the Cold War, an Indian sense of vulnerability was intensified by US pressure to roll back its nuclear weapons programme. Sensing that nuclear ambivalence was no longer a viable policy and that it was at a policy crossroads, India broke out of what its leaders viewed as a tightening non-proliferation straitjacket and carried out a series of nuclear tests in 1998.[5] After a short period of exasperated criticism and sanctions, the United States relented. The impact of the tests was to enhance India's sense of security (though there were unanticipated repercussions to follow) and endow it with the symbols of power that convinced Washington that New Delhi would be a reliable partner for hedging against a rising China. Other states, including Japan, followed suit and suddenly India was being viewed as an 'emerging power'.[6] This new recognition played into the reawakening of Indian elites' image of their country as one destined to be a major power.

The gathering pace of economic growth produced a sense of national confidence. India's gross domestic product (GDP), which had averaged at just 3 to 4 per cent in the decades after independence, grew to around 7 to 8 per cent each year in the 2000s. In 2007, a Goldman Sachs report predicted that India's economy would overtake that of Japan by 2030 and that of the United States by about 2040.[7] In 2011, India's GDP in purchasing power parity (PPP) terms overtook that of Japan.[8] This is an India too that has weathered numerous difficulties ranging from poverty, slow growth and corruption to serious social conflicts arising from differences in class, caste, religion, gender and language; and that has sustained a democracy that, for all its flaws, has embedded itself in the national consciousness.[9] Despite the tumult, India's democracy has worked well enough for its citizens not to worry about national survival.

The surge in Indian material power and self-confidence together facilitated a remarkably rapid shift from India's old tendency to keep the dominant normative order at arm's length to a new determination to conform to it and, further, to attain a high social position within it. To a large extent, India's world view was transformed from that of a defensive, prickly state to one that today articulates the ambition to become a 'leading power'.[10] Even so, India retained a significant non-conformist element. For instance, as we will argue below, India refused to become a signatory to the NPT, continued to champion developing-country interests in specific areas such as climate change; and shied away from the growing 'Responsibility to Protect' (R2P) norm in cases of human rights violation.

Dominant material associations and international norms in the post-Cold War era

Following the end of the Cold War, material power has remained central, yet this centrality has been eroded by states' perceived need to cooperate on substantive issues. Economic power, while constrained by interdependence, continues to be a status marker and one which has given high status to a newly minted major power (China) and 'rising' status to several emerging powers (such as Brazil, India and South Africa). Military power remains central to status, underlined by widely circulated data on who spends how much and on what. However, nuclear weapons are a mixed bag. In the aftermath of the Cold War, the United States and Russia brought their weapons stocks down significantly, especially through the Strategic Arms Reduction Treaty (START I, 1994) and the New START Treaty (2011). Yet the process, which at one time seemed to augur forward movement on complete disarmament, lost momentum as US–Russia tensions increased dramatically over NATO expansion, missile defence, Moscow's intervention in Ukraine, and other issues.

The structuring norms of the Cold War described in Chapter 2 faded away at the beginning of this period and brought initial optimism that, in Hegelian terms, the 'end of history' had arrived, that is, that there would be no more fundamental ideational conflict.[11] But new complexities emerged quickly. Al Qaeda's targeting of Washington, China's resistance to US power in East Asia, Russia's challenge to the United States in Ukraine, and nuclear tests by India, Pakistan and North Korea shattered the US grand design. Not only did the alliance politics of yesteryear unravel, but the new era began to fundamentally reshape major power politics. Although it appeared that a new balance of power was in the making, with the United States, Japan and India ranged against China, Russia and Pakistan, this was not alliance politics. In the unfolding age of 'strategic partnerships', there was little commitment among the major powers to back their partners' disputes; no partnership spelt out who it was aimed at; and – above all – most major players had strong economic stakes in strategic adversaries.[12]

Among the dominant systemic norms, global economic integration based on Adam Smith's germinal thought has progressed and remains a strong idea, but has been restrained by the formation of competitive blocs such as the North American Free Trade Association (NAFTA) and the Asia Pacific Economic Cooperation forum (APEC). Larger 'mega-FTAs' such as the Trans-Pacific Partnership (TPP), the Trans-Atlantic Trade and Investment Partnership (TTIP) and the Regional Comprehensive Economic Partnership (RCEP), though controversial, have begun to take shape.[13] Other developing norms have similarly made significant but limited advances. The democracy norm has gathered strength globally with more and more authoritarian states adopting democratic systems of governance. One specific aspect – human rights protection – has seen remarkable growth: following military interventions for humanitarian purposes in Haiti and Kosovo in the 1990s, the UN-endorsed global political commitment of R2P has legitimised international sanctions and military intervention to safeguard human rights.[14] However, R2P as a principle has periodically run into political trouble over military interventions, notably in Libya and Syria. The cooperative norm on mitigation and adaption in the face of climate change has, with the support of most major powers (despite US reluctance), made some progress, though, owing to competing national interests, a strong collective response is yet to emerge.[15] Global norms, as with the distribution of global power, have thus been in considerable flux.

Associational status seeking in the post-Cold War era

Since states are regularly motivated by security considerations in accumulating military power, it is not easy to separate their pursuit of power from status-seeking motives. In addition, states that are integrated – or in the process of integrating – with the global system of economic exchange and are expanding their international economic activities, tend to enhance their military power, and especially their power projection capabilities, in order to protect their interests.[16] One key outcome of a state's acquisition of power is that its potential to raise its status increases, provided it satisfies our third source of status attainment: conformity with prevailing norms. Below, we examine the post-Cold War India story along these lines.

Material attributes

As we have seen, military defeat in 1962 prompted a concerted effort to acquire military power, with visible results by the late 1980s. From the 1990s, the shift to a liberalising economy contributed to a quickening rate of growth, which had been on the upswing from the early 1980s.[17] This in turn permitted the development of a stronger military. India's quest for status now rested on a foundation of material power.

Economic power

India's centralised, state-dominated economic system with its large public sector had restrained economic growth. The balance of payments crisis that coincided with the end of the Cold War compelled India to make 'structural adjustments' as required by the IMF. This meant significant deregulation and opening up the economy to market forces. Prime Minister P. V. Narasimha Rao and his finance minister (later prime minister) Manmohan Singh went beyond the expectations of the IMF and ushered in extensive changes, setting in motion the dismantlement of the much criticised 'license permit raj' that had hitherto stifled the economy and hampered growth.[18]

India's expanded economy has not only brought status recognition as a major economic player, but has enabled it to enhance its role as a provider of foreign economic assistance (though not comparable to China or the United States), a remarkable change for a country better known as a major aid recipient for much of its independent history. Total allocation for what India terms 'development cooperation' in 2015/16 under its two main categories – Technical and Economic Cooperation, and Loans and Advances to Foreign Governments – amounted to about $1.33 billion.[19] Much of this assistance is focused on India's poorest neighbours in South Asia, but substantial commitments have also been made to Africa and elsewhere. As many as twenty-three states receiving Indian aid have a higher per capita GDP than India, which speaks to India's efforts to open markets and more generally gain influence and hence status.[20]

Military power

In the preceding chapter, we showed how, by the 1980s, India had become a significant military power in the Indian Ocean region. In the post-Cold War period, India has focused on consolidating its position as a maritime power in the Indian Ocean and on slowly extending its influence further, particularly eastward to Southeast Asia and the Western Pacific. All of the three services – the army, the air force and the navy – have received major injections of finance aimed at modernising their often obsolete equipment.[21] India's annual military spending has grown from $7.99 billion in 1991 to $47.95 billion in 2015.[22] Expenditure on the import of weapons has been particularly large. For the period 2010–14, India was the world's largest recipient of arms transfers.[23] In relative terms, this phenomenal growth has not been unduly burdensome: military spending as a percentage of GDP has *declined* from 2.9 per cent in 1991 to 2.2 per cent in 2015.[24] The emphasis has been on quality rather than quantity. For the same years, the numbers in terms of military personnel or major weapons platforms have not changed much (except combat aircraft, which have increased from 674 in 1991 to 881 in 2015).[25]

India's acquisition of arms has been criticised as lacking a clear and comprehensive political and military strategy. As Stephen Cohen and Sunil Dasgupta have shown, the massive acquisition of weapons has not been accompanied by concerted efforts to develop appropriate doctrine and organisational capacity.[26] While India has underlined restraint in its strategic behaviour, a substantial portion of the weapons acquired (an additional aircraft carrier, for example) 'suggest power projection rather than restraint'.[27] But the apparent puzzle is not a puzzle at all if we recognise that in good part what India is conceivably aiming at is *symbolic*: its weapons systems are not only for use in armed conflict, but also for display as accoutrements of power. This is underlined by our analysis later in this chapter of India's emphasis on the non-use of force.

Nuclear power

The point becomes more obvious when we look at India's nuclear capabilities. India currently deploys some 54 ballistic missiles and is in the process of developing and acquiring a range of air-, land- and sea-based launchers.[28] On the one hand, New Delhi abides by a strategy of 'minimum deterrence' that stresses No First Use (NFU), eschews active deployment and favours universal nuclear disarmament; on the other, it has set in motion a research and development programme that bears the hallmarks of Cold War arms competition. The Indian missile programme encompasses a wide range of short-, medium- and long-range missiles, including the Agni-VI missile (currently with a 6,000-km range but planned for a 10,000-km range[29]), a variety of delivery vehicles, and multiple-warhead missiles. While there may indeed be other motivations at work, such as the organisational interests of missile producers, it is hard not to infer that status considerations are a part of policy makers' motives.

Ironically, the status motive has received a boost from Washington. Although US officials do not publicly admit it, their interest in India as a strategic, rather than simply an economic partner became serious only after its 1998 nuclear tests. The point was made obliquely by US secretary of state Condoleezza Rice, who told the Senate Foreign Relations Committee in April 2006 that India is a 'rising power' that will 'continue to possess sophisticated military forces ...'.[30] While nuclear capability does not automatically enhance status, as suggested by Pakistan's failed efforts to obtain concessions on civilian nuclear trade from the non-proliferation regime,[31] there is little doubt that India's nuclear capability, along with its economic revival and its democratic system, was instrumental in cementing the India–US strategic partnership. That lesson appears to be incorporated in India's apparently dysfunctional weapons policy. India is not 'arming without aiming', as Cohen and Dasgupta argue; its aims just encompass more than the usual security ones.

Relations with the dominant powers

In contrast to its orientation until the end of the 1980s, post-Cold War India's strategy began with its acceptance of the main structures of political and economic power within the international system. India embraced the dominant systemic norms of hard power primacy and liberal capitalism. While these were essential to Indian economic and military security, they also carried opportunities for status advancement. Accordingly, Indian policy makers have introduced key changes to their foreign policy framework.

First, India has largely dropped its efforts to bypass major powers and build alternative pathways to influence in global politics. Most prominently, Indian leaders have downgraded their country's involvement in and instrumental use of NAM as an avenue for international leadership. Instead, they have plunged into the politics of the dominant powers by means of a strategic partnership with the United States that, while aimed at tackling the long-term threat both perceive from China, also seeks the status that attends favour from the world's pre-eminent state. With India, the United States has 'play[ed] midwife to the birth of a new power',[32] both materially and socially. India has also abandoned the Cold War-era effort to build a 'New International Economic Order', which envisaged greater equity between the developed world or 'North' and the developing countries of the 'South' by means of improved North–South terms of trade, greater South–South cooperation, and the transfer of finance and technology from the rich to the poor countries. Instead, it is comfortable with a place in the Group of 20 major economies (G20), a club of governments and central bank governors representing nineteen countries plus the European Union and created in 1999, which combines the developed and more advanced developing economies. It has joined hands with efforts to generate new sources of multilateral economic power such as the BRICS Bank and the Asian Infrastructure Investment Bank. The latter includes most developed countries. These institutions allow India to position itself as a major though not top-ranked player in the world economy. India's growing economic power has enabled it to play a prominent role in shaping the rules of international trade through the World Trade Organization.[33] It has also been willing to negotiate preferential and free trade agreements with its neighbours in South and Southeast Asia, and is currently knocking on the doors of the Asia Pacific Economic Cooperation (APEC) bloc.

Second, India has turned sharply from defending its security by keeping the great powers out of its neighbourhood, to being comfortable with such a presence, even inviting it in when the need arises. In the past, Indian leaders were vocal in their criticism of the basing of US forces on the Indian Ocean island of Diego Garcia; now they no longer speak critically of the base. Formerly, India backed a proposal to label the Indian Ocean as a 'zone of peace' in order to keep the United States at bay; today, the idea is aimed at keeping China out.[34] In the 1980s, India had been critical of the US presence in Afghanistan; today, it welcomes this presence. Indeed, in 2002, the Indian Navy escorted US Navy ships participating in Operation Enduring Freedom in Afghanistan.[35] Furthermore, India has actively encouraged a US presence in its immediate environs: it has tried since the early 2000s to persuade Washington to pressurise Pakistan to end its alleged support of cross-border terrorism. In short, India no longer fights shy of major power politics. On the contrary, it participates vigorously in it.

India does so by means of a strategy of networking. In a world where every state's interactions with most others have intensified, a well-chosen networking strategy carries considerable potential for climbing the hierarchical ladder of international society. The networking approach – or the building of social capital – has been a key aspect of the Indian search for high status. In the preceding periods, as we have seen, it was focused on building relationships with other weak states; now, it concentrates primarily on existing and aspiring major powers. At its centre lies the forging of multiple strategic partnerships with major as well as minor powers.[36] The aims of these partnerships vary, but the main ones (with major powers other than China) contain security-seeking and status-seeking dimensions and, additionally, avenues for building economic cooperation. Their interactions include capability building through arms transfers as well as cooperative security practices such as regular discussions on matters of mutual interest, joint exercises, training, and joint or coordinated patrols. It is sometimes asked: what is the purpose of such diverse and numerous strategic partnerships?[37] For India, the advantage of such partnerships is that they provide for flexibility, focus on positive areas of cooperation, do not entail deep commitments, help avoid entrapment in partners' disputes with other states, and, above all, provide space for strategic autonomy.[38] Is this an updated form of nonaligned strategy or 'Nonalignment 2.0'[39]? In a sense, yes: such partnerships allow states to avoid putting all their strategic eggs in one basket. As Prime Minister Singh expressed it in a 2005 address, a pillar of his strategy was 'to seek partnerships, both on the strategic front and on the economic and technological front, that widen our policy and developmental options'.[40] From the social capital perspective, networks provide pathways to making connections and building coalitions that enable India to garner the all-round influence and esteem that are vital for enhancing status.

Close interaction with major and second-level powers is part of a wider networking strategy which India has employed over the years to attain a position in regional and global multilateral groupings. The former include the Indian Ocean Rim Association, the Shanghai Cooperation Organization and the East Asia Summit; the latter encompass the G20, BRICS (Brazil, Russia, India, China, South Africa) and IBSA (India, Brazil, South Africa). Unlike its relationships with major powers, these smaller networks do not directly offer anything of substance by way of capability building (Russia excepted). But they do involve active participation for diverse purposes: political mobilisation for memberships in key institutions, strategic connections relating to balance-of-power interests, and ensuring that the policies adopted by these institutions do not militate against Indian interests. In short, these second-level groupings complement the networks involving the big players.

The status benefits of this networking approach are considerable. It is an approach that builds on India's recent accumulation of material power while drawing India closer to key players in the power hierarchy. The chief source of status gains for India in the post-Cold War era has been without doubt the United States, particularly after the accession to power of President George W. Bush in 2001. Less concerned about nuclear proliferation than his predecessor Bill Clinton, Bush was proactive in cultivating Indian prime ministers Atal Bihari Vajpayee and Manmohan Singh, and his administration declared that its goal was 'to help India become a major world power in the 21st century'.[41] The warming relationship led to extensive military cooperation and major arms purchases that signalled that India had, in effect, arrived as a significant player that would shape the future of Asian and indeed global politics.[42] Nothing underlined India's new relationship with the United States more dramatically than Bush's willingness, announced by an initial agreement in 2005, to help India break out of the constraints imposed on it by the nuclear non-proliferation regime and to allow it to engage in civilian nuclear commerce (on which more below).

Japan, too, has drawn close to India and the nomenclature of 'special and strategic global partnership' accorded to their relationship underlines the importance both give to it. In a significant breakthrough, a major hurdle was crossed when Japan agreed in November 2011 to undertake civil nuclear commerce with India. There appears to be an informal India–Japan–US triangular partnership in the offing.[43] Following trilateral meetings among India, Japan and Australia in June 2015 and among India, Japan and the US in the same September, it would appear that the idea of a 'democratic quadrilateral', which proved to be short-lived in 2007, is being quietly rekindled, which makes India a key player in the increasingly Asia-centric international system.[44]

Specific interests aside, the overall thrust of India's networking diplomacy is to obtain seats at multiple tables, old and new. An important status marker is the United Nations Security Council (UNSC) and India has actively pursued UN reform and laid claim to permanent membership of the Council.[45] Interestingly, Indian representatives at the UN first made a formal bid for a permanent seat on the Council in 1994, at a time of economic, political and regional turbulence, and when India had just lost its Cold War insurance of Soviet support.[46] Certainly, then, India's bid for permanent membership of the Security Council did not issue from a position of material power. Its success has been limited thus far, but that is hardly unexpected, given the broader complexities of Council reform.[47] More to the point, the very process of obtaining support for the objective has enabled India to generate the image of a major power in the making. India has joined hands with fellow-claimants: it is a member of the informal Group of Four (G4) along with Brazil, Germany and Japan. All the major powers other than China have been supportive of India, which in itself has enhanced the credibility of Indian status claims. A large number of other countries have supported India's bid (though the thirteen members of the group known as Uniting for Consensus have not[48]), which in turn has helped build its image as a legitimate candidate for permanent membership of the UNSC as well as a potential major power.

Finally, a closer look at India's networking strategy reveals its status-seeking priority. India has not played a major role or displayed much initiative in many of the networks of institutions of which it is part, but appears content with occupying a seat at the table. At the Security Council, India was elected president in 2010, but its performance with respect to major crises in Côte d'Ivoire, Libya and Syria was unimpressive.[49] India's lacklustre involvement in regional deliberations was emphasised by Defence Minister A. K. Anthony's absence in 2013 from a Singapore forum attended by senior statespersons from major powers – the Shangri-La Dialogue – even though he was present in the city at the time. In the same year, Anthony failed to attend the ASEAN Defence Ministers Meeting (ADMM) as well as an ASEAN meeting in Brunei.[50] The experience in IONS has not been much better. Having initiated the forum, India appears to have done little to invigorate it.[51] This evidence thus suggests that to date, India's primary interest is in the attainment of status through institutional membership in and of itself, rather than expending efforts to use its position constructively once membership has been obtained.

Normative status seeking in the post-Cold War era

As we have seen, a key dimension of status seeking is the way in which a state responds to prevailing norms, which are largely established by the major powers. In this section, we examine India's responses to dominant global norms through the limited legacies of India's earlier counter-order efforts, India's engagement with the non-proliferation regime, and status gains arising from India's standing as a liberal democracy and its fuller post-Cold War integration into the global economy. We also look at an additional aspect of its status-seeking strategy: India's contribution to the stability of the system – an expected form of 'status enactment' – through its application of military power for the public good without the actual use of force. This is in line with the positive notion of a 'good'[52] or 'responsible'[53] power that contributes to the stability of the international system. However, the Indian approach to status enactment today does not extend to forms of burden-sharing that require the deployment of the use of force. In the customary view, great powers 'are expected to act differently from other states and, especially, to be involved in more alliances, more conflicts, and more conflicts further from their home territories'.[54] That India has not joined any alliance may reflect its non-aligned history, but it is also in tune with more recent global history: in the post-Cold War world, there are no new alliances, and those that remain, notably the North Atlantic Treaty Organisation (NATO), have a much more limited role than in the past. Instead, major and minor powers alike forge 'strategic partnerships', which, if anything, are inclined to avoid conflicts. A more creative aspect of India's drive for status is that it seeks respect and wide acceptability by *not* intervening militarily in neighbouring countries or farther afield and by restricting itself to the peaceful uses of military power.

Responses to dominant global norms

In the post-Nehru era, as we demonstrated in the preceding chapter, India adopted a counter-order strategy through the cultivation and fortification of the Non-Aligned Movement. While the grouping's central rationale – to remain apart from both the Soviet and the US-led blocs – appeared redundant with the ending of the Cold War, the stripped-back essence of the Movement – to retain the autonomy of its members in world affairs and to resist 'imperialism' – has remained alive, even if some argue that the Movement has 'long outlived its mission and usefulness'.[55]

Prime Minister Rao certainly retained faith in the NAM in the wake of the end of the Cold War. In the lead up to the Tenth Non-Aligned Summit held at Jakarta in September 1992 – the first non-aligned summit at heads of state and government level following the collapse of the Soviet Union – Rao anticipated 'a more competition-prone and hegemonic situation' rather than a 'benign unipolar phenomenon'.[56] Indian foreign policy elites quickly realised in the wake of the 1991 Gulf War that the United States was 'becoming the most potent political and military power in the world',[57] and that a newly political and militarily intrusive role for the United Nations, in particular the Security Council, was being designed and promoted by the United States and its allies.[58] Rao approached the Jakarta Summit with the intention of recalibrating the NAM agenda to tackle the changed international situation and its new challenges. A hectic programme of ministerial visits by India to important non-aligned countries in the lead up to the Summit sought to secure 'some cohesion and purposiveness' among key member states 'because a great deal of covert pressure was being exerted by Western governmental and academic circles to wind up the movement'.[59] The final documents of the Jakarta Summit acknowledged momentous shifts in the world order – both positive and negative – but stressed that the world was 'still far from being a peaceful, just and secure place'.[60] In the wake of the Jakarta Summit, and with significant input from India, NAM members would generate momentum for the reform of the United Nations, including opening up formal discussions over the issue of Security Council reform.[61]

However, even as the NAM has shifted to issuing an array of challenges to the 'liberal hegemony of the West' as opposed to 'the bipolarity of the Cold War', arguably, the Movement has struggled to prove its relevance.[62] Indeed, in 2016, controversy reigned within and beyond India as Prime Minister Modi was accused of 'skipping' the 17th Non-Aligned Summit in Margarita, Venezuela. Some read his absence as a monumental snub to the Movement and as confirmation that it was in its death throes.[63] However, a high-profile diplomatic replacement was dispatched to Margarita in Modi's absence, underscoring the continued significance of the Movement to India, and on closer inspection, Modi's absence itself appeared more linked to banal scheduling problems than to a deliberate downplaying of the grouping's significance.[64] The 17th Summit showed that NAM continues to issue compelling critiques of the global order, and remains, with a 120-plus membership, second only to the United Nations in size. The affiliation appears to be worth keeping, since India continues to share interests with NAM members across issue areas such as UN reform, peacekeeping, trade negotiations, and even climate change, but also because of India's unique, potentially status-enhancing, and practically useful positioning as a nation now ever more invested in the liberal world order, but equally still attuned to the Movement's criticism of that same order.[65]

This unique positioning also plays out within negotiations over the terms of world trade. Charalampos Efstathopoulos has argued that it is not simply India's status as an emerging economy that has positioned it, together with Brazil, at the centre of Doha round negotiations at the WTO, but also India's (and Brazil's) legitimacy as a representative of the global South. India's leadership strategy at the WTO has been geared to accommodating the 'expectations and preferences' of a developing country followership, and has sought, though with limited success, 'to promote a form of developmental multilateralism that might correct the perceived imbalances within the substantive commitments to and structure and processes of the WTO'.[66]

India's earlier solidarity with G77 countries on climate change, however, has posed ever greater challenges. International discussions and negotiations over environmental issues, including climate change, gained momentum after 1992, and while divisions and alliances within and between the North and South blocs were always commonplace, in general terms, the South united around a belief in its member's collective minimal historical contributions to environmental damage, limited threat posed given a scenario of inaction, and reduced capacity to mitigate environmental damage. Today, however, India, along with a handful of other states, has emerged as an important exception to much of this Southern framing, due to the expansion of its population, economy and market: in 2012 India ranked, after the United States, China and the European Union, as the fourth largest carbon emitter.[67] The 2009 United Nations Climate Change Conference, held in Copenhagen, signalled a clear Indian move away from a stance typically associated with other countries in the G77, after a new China-led bloc emerged, comprising four large developing countries – China, India, South Africa and Brazil – the BASIC grouping. These countries have sought to resist increasing pressure from developed and developing countries alike to curb their emissions, and to carve out a deal on the climate that reflects many of their persistent commonalities with developing countries, including the onus placed on resisting limitations to development. India can, however, no longer credibly claim solidarity with much of the developing world on the issue of climate change.

Even as the 2015 Paris Accord, which India signed and then ratified in late 2016, largely safeguards the principle of common but differentiated responsibilities that has been at the heart of India's negotiating stance for decades, the framing of the Accord leaves a question mark over what precisely the international community will consider India's future responsibilities to be.

A final aspect of the post-Cold war normative order that has met with Indian resistance has been the emerging norm of the Responsibility to Protect (R2P), which embodies a global political commitment to prevent mass human rights abuses including genocide, war crimes, and ethnic cleansing. India has offered reluctant support to R2P, although, as one analyst underscores, it

> remains highly sceptical about pillar three, which establishes the right to intervention in the internal affairs of a sovereign state if such state is unwilling or unable to protect its population, and particularly rejects the use of military means in this context.[68]

Indian arguments are built on both principle and anxiety, embodying a judgment on what India sees as the historically self-interested interventionist tendencies of Western powers, and fears over India's own vulnerabilities to outside interference given internal conflicts and challenges.[69] At the root of the Indian stance on R2P is a reluctance to endorse the use of force as a means of resolving conflicts; a recognition that interventions are costly, often have unintended and unpredictable consequences, and cannot in and of themselves ensure the establishment of ensuing democratic governance; and an enduring suspicion of major Western powers and their motives in seeking to intervene militarily for humanitarian purposes.[70]

Non-proliferation

A quest which has been predominant in Indian foreign policy since the mid-1990s has been entry into the hitherto barred halls of the nuclear non-proliferation regime. While power is generally a prerequisite for status, India's motivation in this case is different. While all of the permanent members of the UNSC, who are coincidentally the only nuclear-armed powers recognised as 'Nuclear-Weapon States' under the NPT, are members of the regime's institutions – most prominently the Nuclear Suppliers Group (NSG) – so are several other lesser powers. The NSG is not an elite club. Indian interest in it is driven by a sense of being discriminated against, a derivative perception of the way

Indians have viewed the NPT since its inception, and to which the NSG is closely linked.

Entry into the main institutions of the nuclear non-proliferation regime represents a special case with respect to India's quest for status. As we have seen, India refrained from actively pursuing the bomb and at the same time rejected the NPT as discriminatory. Since 1998, having conducted a series of nuclear tests and declared itself a nuclear power, India has expended considerable diplomatic energy on seeking membership of the various institutional components of the non-proliferation regime, primarily the NSG (which restricts commerce in nuclear materials and technology), the Missile Technology Control Regime (MTCR, which regulates the transfer of missile-related materials and technology) and the Wassenaar Arrangement (which restricts commerce in dual-use technology as well as conventional and cyber technologies).[71] The thrust of its effort has been to relocate itself by moving from the position of an 'outlier' to that of an integral member of the non-proliferation regime.

A significant breakthrough in this respect was achieved when India and the United States in 2008 finalised a bilateral agreement that had been initiated in 2005. The 'nuclear deal' entailed a change in American domestic law to permit the export of civilian nuclear materials and know-how to India without insisting on India's placement of its nuclear facilities under 'full-scope' International Atomic Energy Agency (IAEA) safeguards, a benchmark required by NSG export policy since the early 1990s.[72] The United States went on to persuade the NSG to make an exception for India and agreed in principle to follow suit, though each member state would have to alter its domestic laws individually in order to permit nuclear trade with India. This accommodation gave India an exceptional status as the only non-signatory NPT state known to possess nuclear weapons that has been granted access to civil nuclear trade. The United States also agreed to back India's application for entry into the NSG, the MTCR and the Wassenaar Arrangement. However, objections from China and other smaller states blocked India's ambitions in the NSG, though India gained entry into the MTCR (of which China was not a member) in June 2016. At the time of writing (late 2016), India's application for NSG membership is still pending owing to opposition from some members, primarily China. New Delhi has shown both persistence and patience in its pursuit of membership.

India has gone to great lengths to portray itself as a 'responsible nuclear power', that is – as we explain in the introduction – a power that enacts its status by conforming to the dominant norm of nuclear non-proliferation.[73] An early official expression of the claim to being responsible was in the immediate aftermath of India's 1998 nuclear tests, when the government's defence of its actions was placed in the context not only of strategic need, but was also asserted in language that emphasised India's sound non-proliferation record as a 'responsible state possessing nuclear weapons'.[74] India's claim eventually earned US acknowledgment when President Bush, in a joint statement with Prime Minister Singh, signalled appreciation of India's commitment to non-proliferation and affirmed that India was a 'responsible state with advanced nuclear technology'.[75] This recognition, repeatedly stated by US policy makers, was an important additional justification employed for responding to opposition to the India–US nuclear deal.[76] From India's standpoint, its accommodation by the regime was an important breakthrough that elevated its status from a virtual pariah to a nuclear weapons power, though not a 'Nuclear-Weapon State' as defined by the NPT.[77]

Democracy and the liberal economic order

Severe constraints notwithstanding, the Indian state has managed to sustain a democratic political framework throughout the decades since Independence. The period from the mid-1980s to 2014 was particularly challenging as the decline of the once-dominant Congress Party brought an era of often short-lived coalition governments at the centre. Yet the overall sense of stability remained in spite of a host of problems ranging from poverty to secessionist movements.[78] The 1991 turn to market-oriented economic policies had clearly ended state-dominated development and turned India into a liberal-capitalist democracy. This created a new image of India among the US-led dominant powers as having become, in effect, 'one of them' rather than a challenger to the status quo as it had long been.

Dominant international norms are by and large those established by powerful states. The norm of liberal democracy was greatly strengthened by the end of the Cold War, after having survived challenges from Hitler's Germany, the Soviet Union, and the idea of the Third World (in the last case, the economic aspect of 'liberal' democracy had been widely questioned). India's conformity with this norm has been a source of much advantage to it. Claims about the success of the Indian democratic experiment appeal to both Western liberal democracies, particularly as liberal political architecture has gained currency in the post-Cold war global order, and to other states and societies in transition for whom India is deemed to stand as a model. In 2005, Prime Minister Singh could claim with some satisfaction that 'the world looks to us in the practice of democracy. We are a unique example of a developing country of such great diversity seeking its salvation through the framework of an open society and a functioning democracy'.[79]

In particular, India's democracy has been successfully exploited by the United States to pursue the cultivation of India as a strategic partner. This was most evident in the run-up to the India–US nuclear agreement of 2008, which involved much hard bargaining with domestic opponents of the Bush proposal to make an exception for India and change the rules of nuclear commerce. The US decision to tilt strongly toward India was justified by Under Secretary of State R. Nicholas Burns with the assertion that 'like the United States, India will thrive as a multi-ethnic, multi-religious and multi-lingual democracy, characterized by individual freedom, rule of law and a constitutional government that owes its power to free and fair elections'.[80] Senate Foreign Relations Committee chairman Richard Lugar echoed this view: 'We need more from India than security cooperation. We need a partner that sits at the intersection of several strategic regions and that can be a bulwark for stability, democracy, and pluralism'.[81] Robert Blackwill, ambassador to India and a key architect of the policy, noted that, even before becoming president, Bush himself was deeply attracted to India for the same reason:

> When I asked then-Governor Bush in early 1999 about the reasons for his obvious and special interest in India, he immediately responded, 'a billion people in a functioning democracy. Isn't that something? Isn't that something?'[82]

On the nuclear exception for India, arguing for a discriminating policy on non-proliferation, Secretary of State Rice observed in her testimony before the Senate Foreign Relations Committee that India, a democracy, could not be bracketed with non-democracies like Iran and North Korea.[83]

Thus India's democratic character played an essential part in the Bush administration's argument for overriding the strong non-proliferation lobby in the United States. India further strengthened this bond by joining hands with the US to launch the 'Community of Democracies' and also became a leading donor to the UN Democracy Fund, which supports civil society participation in governance.[84] Nonetheless, India has been cautious about propagating democracy. Its reservations about intervening forcefully in the cause of human rights and democracy promotion stem from the potential difficulties involved and from its own vulnerability to claims that it resorts to repression in responding to domestic political opposition.

On the negative side, Indian politics has produced a degree of right-wing extremism that has raised questions regarding the country's democratic credentials. In particular, since 2014 under Modi's leadership, violence against religious minorities, assaults on women, an inordinate and sometimes violent focus on the prohibition of beef consumption, and crackdowns on political dissent have begun to generate an image of weakening democracy.[85] In the face of this, Modi has nonetheless continued to celebrate India's democracy, if not explicitly its pluralism, on the international stage. In September 2014, in a prominent interview with Fareed Zakaria on CNN (who hosted Modi and Bill Clinton on the same show), Modi stressed that 'democracy is our commitment. It is our great legacy, a legacy we simply cannot compromise. Democracy is in our DNA'.[86] So far, India's global image as a liberal democracy has survived and continues to contribute to its rising status.

Where India's economic liberal credentials are concerned, as seen earlier, India's resistance to integration with the global economy was driven by concerns that its weak economy would fall prey to the structural inequality believed to be perpetrated by 'neocolonialism'. The shock of the 1991 balance of payments crisis triggered a drastic shift. The idea of a New International Economic Order was abandoned and India began to dismantle its highly restrictive system of economic regulation in both its internal and external dimensions. Finance Minister Singh, the architect of the reforms, was convinced that India should welcome rather than resist foreign investment and that 'we must not remain permanent captives of a fear of the East India Company, as if nothing has changed in the past 300 years'.[87]

Trade, long minimised by the desire to escape the marginalisation thought to be intrinsic to a neocolonial centre–periphery system, became increasingly integral to the economy. India's foreign trade as a proportion of GDP grew from 17 per cent in 1991 to 49 per cent in 2014.[88] Foreign Direct Investment (FDI), long shunned as the harbinger of exploitation by the capitalist centre, expanded rapidly: net FDI inflows grew from a meagre $73.53 million in 1991 to $44.20 billion in 2015. The infusion of technology along with finance was a tonic for India's stagnating economy. The liberalisation process was less turbulent than many critics anticipated and the pace of economic development picked up.

Status enactment and the use of force

Historically, major powers have from time to time used force to impose order (in their own interests, of course). In the past, as seen in Chapter 3,

India has had occasion to do so from time to time, whether on invitation or otherwise. In the years since the end of the Cold War, Indian military power has grown rapidly, in part owing to the infusion of greater resources made available by faster growth. As noted earlier, many of the new weapons acquisitions are suitable for power projection. Yet India has avoided military action, other than the minimum that is required for UN peacekeeping.[89] We pointed out earlier that, in part, the utility of India's massive induction of advanced weapons lies in their symbolic value, which can contribute to higher status. But there is more to Indian military restraint than that. As Iver Neumann has observed, states may take an approach to status that focuses on 'the symbolic resource of exemplary behaviour according to some civilizational standard'.[90] In attempting to enact the status that India has accrued as a rising power, India has sought to demonstrate its commitment to order. It has gone some way to doing this by contributing to bilateral and multilateral efforts to maintain order through defence cooperation. India has also been active in making available its armed forces for humanitarian assistance, notably in the aftermath of the tsunami disaster of 2004.[91]

India's efforts to promote itself as a 'net security provider' have been restricted to three kinds of activity.[92] First, Indian forces have focused on protecting the commons, which has involved deploying naval ships against piracy in the western Indian Ocean and escorting American and other ships across the Indian Ocean. Second, India has played a major role in HADR (Humanitarian Assistance and Disaster Relief) missions, as in post-tsunami operations in South and Southeast Asia in 2004–2005, and in the evacuation of civilians from war-torn Yemen in March-April 2015. And third, it has provided military assistance in the form of military equipment and training to a number of countries, most prominently Afghanistan and Vietnam. But India has refrained from two types of potentially costly action that might be assumed key to the enactment of its emerging status: unilateral military intervention in trouble spots, and invited involvement in zones of conflict.

Examples of Indian restraint abound. In 2003, the United States formally requested India to send a brigade-strength 'stabilisation force' to Iraq, but India declined.[93] A few years later, India played a half-hearted role – by way of unpublicised military aid to Colombo – in Sri Lanka's final thrust to defeat the Liberation Tigers of Tamil Eelam (LTTE), a terrorist group that Indian military forces had unsuccessfully fought in the late 1980s.[94] India has major strategic interests and eco-nomic investments in Afghanistan, yet has not only resisted sending military forces there, but been extraordinarily hesitant to deliver military aid.[95] These, critics may well say, are signs of a reluctance on the part of India to enact its growing status in costly ways, with the result that India generates an image contrary to its search for recognition as a major player in the international system.[96] What is India trying to do? Is it trying to achieve higher status on the cheap? That may well be part of the answer. The experience of the Indian peacekeeping force in Sri Lanka in the late 1980s was a signal lesson on the costs of intervention. However, post-war Indian foreign policy discourse, perhaps less so under the Modi government, has tended to emphasise the distinctiveness of India's intended role as its rises. An analysis of elite discourse centring on India's global role finds that,

> Despite India's increasing economic power and military might, Indian conceptions of the kinds of state behaviour deemed appropriate and legitimate continue to be set in contrast to those of the 'Western powers' of the twentieth and early twenty-first centuries, where a key marker of this distinction is a persistent Indian reluctance to enter into military alliances and interfere in the affairs of other states.[97]

In this sense, India is also seeking to provide public goods – or enact higher status – in a manner that distinguishes itself from the heavy-handedness of the major powers. Such a strategy of innovation, albeit limited innovation, removes a great deal of controversy and criticism from the perspective of states with equivalent or lower status than India, who are a key part of India's networking strategy.

Has the rise of Prime Minister Narendra Modi, leader of a political party – the Bharatiya Janata Party (BJP) – widely dubbed 'Hindu nationalist', brought a change to India's conformity with dominant norms regarding the use of force? Some argue that the BJP and Modi represent a tougher, more muscular approach to foreign policy associated with the embrace of nuclear weapons and a harder stance toward China and Pakistan.[98] To an extent this may be true: Modi has not worried about China's response to India's warming relationship with Japan, for instance. But a closer look reveals that he has essentially built on embedded older norms and practices described in these pages and elsewhere: integration with the global economy and power, building military capability, networking for status (and security), and military restraint.[99] More fundamentally, the BJP's notion of power, which goes back to the 1920s, reflects a desire for power to *defend* the nation rather than to change the external environment.[100] Modi's basic foreign policy principles of *Panchamrit* (literally, 'five sacred foods') encompasses honor (*sammān*), dialogue (*samvād*), shared prosperity (*samriddhi*), regional and global security (*suraksha*) and cultural and civilisational linkages (*sanskriti evam sabhyata*) – in sum, not a particularly aggressive set of tenets guiding strategic behaviour.[101] His policies therefore represent no significantly new approach to the attainment of either security or status.

Finally, let us return to dominant expectations of status enactment in the contemporary world order. For some, it involves a willingness to sustain that order at some cost – a cost often associated with the use of force, sometimes far from home. That is a risky enterprise for a state with limited resources. For all the enormity of its arms spending, the relative level of India's military expenditure, as we have seen earlier in this chapter, is not very high. Despite its self-confident vision of its future as a major power, India retains a measure of caution about its capabilities. Hence, it is attempting to achieve higher status by means of a cautious low-cost route of status enactment – one that underlines its individual commitment to order, but not a willingness to enforce that commitment upon others. High status in the sense of respect is not just about rank and power; it is also about 'who is endowed with legitimate authority'.[102] India's approach to attaining status aims to renounce the costly use of power in favour of behaviour that demonstrates moral authority. Writing about the status-seeking approach of small states, Neumann and de Carvalho draw our attention to their preference, given their lack of material power, for being seen as 'good' powers while contributing to a stable world order.[103] India is by no means a small state, but, conscious of its many vulnerabilities, and bearing in mind longstanding ideational frameworks that are both averse to the use of force and primed to demonstrate moral superiority, its leaders appear to be following such a strategy, focusing on the cooperative and non-violent delivery of public goods at low cost. India's preference for strategic partnerships, joint patrols, military exercises, peacekeeping and humanitarian missions, and above all for restraint in military action, makes such an approach to status optimal, if at times disappointing to some major powers.

Conclusion

In this chapter, we have argued that India's search for higher status has led it to change tack from a fearful rejection of the power structures of international society to a more confident engagement with these. Having moved after the end of the Cold War to integrate with and adapt to the major power-dominated system, India has experienced significant growth and its leaders have begun to think of their country as having the potential to attain the status of a major power not too far into the future. India's status-seeking strategy since the early 1990s has three main features. The building of material power has enabled it to generate the image of a major power in the making. The economic aspect – rapid growth and the expansion of (still limited) programmes of overseas assistance – has been overshadowed by the more visible traditional symbols of military power: conventional and nuclear weapons. Closer links with the major powers, especially the United States, have given India an increasingly prominent profile in Asian and global politics, with others, notably Japan, also drawn to embrace it. If India's strategy has retained some flavour of the past in the form of non-commitment to alliance making, that resonates well with a practice that has fast become standardised: all states are building strategic partnerships in an age that is conceivably a post-alliance one.

Finally, India has abandoned much of its old proclivity for challenging systemic norms, although its leaders continue to seek common cause with developing countries in the WTO, position their country against developed states and the major powers on climate change, and are highly sceptical of R2P. Largely, however, India is seeking to adapt itself to the dominant norms of the day: liberal democracy, integration with the global capitalist economy, and the enactment of status in ways that contribute to the stability of the system, in particular in the domain of nuclear non-proliferation. However, as against the historical norm of major power behaviour, which has typically involved military intervention (and the willingness to incur the costs that come with it), India has followed a path that emphasises military restraint and application of the soft face of hard power – using its military capability in non-forceful ways. The Indian approach to status seeking has been low-cost, and has focused on demonstrating capability without exercising military coercion. Rather than a cost-bearing approach, India has sought one that emphasises its legitimacy and moral authority. How far this carries the prospect of success in attaining higher status is another matter. Our focus here is on analysing the strategy, not assessing its rewards.

Notes

1 Ganguly, Sumit and Rahul Mukherji, *India since 1980* (Cambridge: Cambridge University Press, 2011); see especially pp. 80–84 and 22–24 in that order.
2 'RBI's Gold Buying Has Its Own Sentimental Value: FM', *Outlook*, 3 November 2009, www.outlookindia.com/newswire/story/rbis-gold-buying-has-its-own-sentimental-value-fm/668864/?next (accessed on 18 November

2016). For a concise account of the crisis, see Bhattacharya, A. K. 'Two Months that Changed India', *Business Standard*, 2 July 2011, www.business-standard.com/article/beyond-business/two-months-that-changed-india -111070200041_1.html (accessed 18 November 2016).

3   Manmohan Singh, cited in: Ramesh, Jairam, *To the Brink and Back: India's 1991 Story* (New Delhi: Rupa, 2015), pp. 45–46.

4   Cohen, Stephen P., *India: Emerging Power* (Washington, DC: Brookings Institution Press, 2001), p. 106; Hoge Jr, James F., 'A Global Power Shift in the Making: Is the United States Ready?' *Foreign Affairs*, vol. 83, no. 4 (July–August 2004), pp. 2–7.

5   Saksena, Jyotika, 'Regime Design Matters: The CTBT and India's Nuclear Dilemma', *Comparative Strategy*, vol. 25, no. 3 (July 2006), pp. 209–229.

6   Cohen, *India: Emerging Power*; Zakaria, Fareed, 'India Rising', *Newsweek*, 5 March 2006, www.newsweek.com/india-rising-106259 (accessed on 2 February 2015).

7   Poddar, Tushar and Eva Yi, 'India's Rising Growth Potential', Economics Paper no. 152, Goldman Sachs, January 2007.

8   Banerji, Devika and Rishi Shah, 'India Overtakes Japan to Become Third-Largest Economy in Purchasing Power Parity', *Economic Times*, 9 April 2012, http://articles.economictimes.indiatimes.com/2012-04-19/news/ 31367838_1_ppp-terms-india-s-gdp-power-parity (accessed on 6 July 2012).

9   Brown, Judith M., *Modern India: The Origins of an Asian Democracy* (Oxford: Oxford University Press, 1994); Kohli, Atul, *The Success of India's Democracy* (Cambridge: Cambridge University Press, 2001).

10 Jaishankar, S., 'India, the United States and China', Fullerton Lecture, International Institute of Strategic Studies, Singapore, 20 July 2015, www. iiss.org/en/events/events/archive/2015-f463/july-636f/fullerton-lecture-ja ishankar-f64e (accessed on 10 January 2016). Jaishankar was at the time India's foreign secretary.

11 Francis Fukuyama, *The End of History and the Last Man* (New York: Free Press, 1992).

12 Nadkarni, Vidya, *Strategic Partnerships in Asia: Balancing without Alliances* (Abingdon and New York: Routledge, 2010).

13 Ji, Xianbai, Pradumna Bickram Rana, Wai-Mun Chia and Changtai Li, 'Economic and Strategic Dimensions of Mega-FTAs: A Perception Survey of Asian Opinion Leaders', Working paper, S. Rajaratnam School of International Studies, Nanyang Technological University, Singapore, 9 December 2016.

14 On R2P, see: International Commission on Intervention and State Sovereignty, *The Responsibility to Protect: Report of the International Commission on Intervention and State Sovereignty* (Ottawa: International Development Research Centre, December 2001).

15 Dimitrov, Radoslav S., 'The Paris Agreement on Climate Change: Behind Closed Doors', *Global Environmental Politics*, vol. 16, no. 3 (August 2016), pp. 1–11.

16 Fordham, Benjamin O., 'Who Wants to Be a Major Power? Explaining the Expansion of Foreign Policy Ambition', *Journal of Peace Research*, vol. 48, no. 5 (2011), pp. 587–603.

17 Nayyar, Deepak, 'Economic Growth in Independent India: Lumbering Elephant or Running Tiger?' *Economic and Political Weekly*, vol. 41, no. 15 (15–21 April 2006), pp. 1451–1458.

18 Mukherji, Rahul, *Globalization and Deregulation: Ideas, Interests and Institutional Change* (New Delhi: Oxford University Press, 2014), pp. 63–107.

19 India, Ministry of External Affairs, *Annual Report 2015–16*, Appendix XVI, p. 347, https://mea.gov.in/Uploads/PublicationDocs/26525_26525_External_Affairs_English_AR_2015-16_Final_compressed.pdf (accessed on 18 November 2016). The dollar sum is approximate. The report provides data in Indian rupees, which have been converted @$1= INR68.

20 Fuchs, Andreas and Krishna Chaitanya Vadlamannati, 'The Needy Donor: An Empirical Analysis of India's Aid Motives', *World Development*, vol. 44 (2013), see note 29, p. 127.

21 Ganguly, Rajat, 'Indian Military Transformation in the Twenty First Century', in Pauline Eadie and Wyn Rees, eds, *The Evolution of Military Power in the West and Asia: Security Policy in the Post-Cold War Era* (Abingdon and New York: Routledge, 2016), pp. 167–188; Joshi, Shashank, *Indian Power Projection: Ambition, Arms and Influence*. Whitehall Papers (London: Royal United Services Institute for Defence and Security Studies, 2015).

22 The 1991 figure is from International Institute for Strategic Studies, *The Military Balance 1992–1993* (London: Brassey's, 1992), p. 220, while the 2015 figure is from International Institute for Strategic Studies, *The Military Balance 2016* (Oxford: Oxford University Press, 2016), p. 486.

23 Stockholm International Peace Research Institute, *SIPRI Yearbook 2015* (Oxford: Oxford University Press, 2015).

24 The 1991 figure is from *Military Balance 1992–1993*, p. 220, while the 2015 figure is from *Military Balance 2016*, p. 486.

25 The 1991 data are taken from *Military Balance 1992–1993*, pp. 131–133, while the 2015 data are from *Military Balance 2016*, pp. 250–256.

26 Cohen, Stephen P. and Sunil Dasgupta, *Arming without Aiming: India's Military Modernization* (New Delhi: Penguin/Viking, 2010).

27 Ibid., p. 26.

28 *Military Balance 2016*, p. 251. For more details, see Kristensen, Hans M. and Robert S. Norris, 'Indian Nuclear Forces, 2015', *Bulletin of the Atomic Scientists*, vol. 71, no. 5 (2015), pp. 77–83.

29 Rout, Hemant Kumar, 'Stage Set for Longer-Range Surya', *New Indian Express*, 18 September 2013, www.newindianexpress.com/states/odisha/Stage-set-for-longer-range-Surya/2013/09/18/article1790125.ece (accessed 22 February 2015). See also: Narang, Vipin, 'Five Myths about India's Nuclear Posture', *Washington Quarterly*, vol. 36, no. 3 (2013), pp. 143–157.

30 'Remarks of Secretary of State Condoleezza Rice at the Senate Foreign Relations Committee on the US–India Civil Nuclear Cooperation Initiative, Wednesday, April 5, 2006', www.globalsecurity.org/wmd/library/congress/2006_h/060405-rice.pdf (accessed on 20 November 2016).

31 Sullivan de Estrada, Kate and Nicholas J. Wheeler, 'Trustworthy Nuclear Sovereigns? India and Pakistan after the 1998 Tests', *Stosunki Międzynarodowe – International Relations*, vol. 52, no. 2 (2016). doi: 10.7366/020909612201614.

32 Luce, Edward, *In Spite of the Gods: The Strange Rise of Modern India* (London: Abacus, 2007).

33 Efstathopoulos, Charalampos, 'Leadership in the WTO: Brazil, India and the Doha development agenda', *Cambridge Review of International Affairs*, vol. 25, no. 2 (2012), pp. 269–293.

34 Erickson, Andrew S., Walter C. Ladwig III and Justin D. Mikolay, 'Diego Garcia and the United States' Emerging Indian Ocean Strategy', *Asian Security*, vol. 6, no. 3 (2010), pp. 231–232; Singh, Abhijit, 'The Indian Ocean Zone of Peace: Reality vs. Illusion', *The Diplomat*, 7 January 2015, http://thediplomat.com/2015/01/the-indian-ocean-zone-of-peace-rea lity-vs- illusion/ (accessed on 8 December 2016).

35 Koshy, Ninan, *Under the Empire: India's New Foreign Policy* (New Delhi: LeftWord Books, 2006), p. 107.

36 Basrur, Rajesh, 'Modi's Foreign Policy Fundamentals: A Trajectory Unchanged', *International Affairs*, vol. 93, no. 1 (2017), pp. 7–26; Kumar, Satish, S. D. Pradhan, Kanwal Sibal, Rahul Bedi and Bidisha Ganguly, *India's Strategic Partners: A Comparative Assessment*, Foundation for National Security Research, New Delhi, November 2011, http://fnsr.org/files/Indias_Strategic.pdf (accessed on 10 February 2015).

37 Panda, Ankit, 'Why Does India Have So Many "Strategic Partners" and No Allies?' *The Diplomat*, 23 November 2013, http://thediplomat.com/2013/11/why-does-india-have-so-many-strategic-partners-and-no-allies/ (accessed on 2 March 2013).

38 Sibal, Kanwal, '"Strategic" Relations Suit India', *Mail Today*, 26 December 2012, http://indiatoday.in/story/strategic-relations-suit-india-india-today/1/239437.html (accessed on 3 February 2015).

39 Khilnani, Sunil, Rajiv Kumar, Pratap Bhanu Mehta, Prakash Menon, Nandan Nilekani, Srinath Raghavan, Shyam Saran and Siddharth Varadarajan, *Nonalignment 2.0: A Foreign and Strategic Policy for India in the 21st Century* (Cybercity: Penguin, 2013).

40 Manmohan Singh, cited in: Baru, Sanjay, *The Accidental Prime Minister: The Making and Unmaking of Manmohan Singh* (New Delhi: Viking, 2014), p. 169.

41 United States, Department of State, 'Background Briefing by Administration Officials on US–South Asia Relations', 25 March 2005, https://2001-2009.state.gov/r/pa/prs/ps/2005/43853.htm (accessed on 20 November 2016).

42 Blank, Stephen, 'The Geostrategic Implications of the Indo-American Strategic Partnership', *India Review*, vol. 6, no. 1 (2007), pp. 1–24.

43 Nagao, Satoru, *Japan, the United States, and India as Key Balancers in Asia*, Center for Strategic and International Studies, Washington, DC, available at www.csis.org/programs/japan-chair/strategic-japan-working-papers (accessed on 23 November 2016).

44 Parameswaran, Prashanth, 'Return of Asia's Quad "Natural": US Defense Chief', *The Diplomat*, 9 April 2016, http://thediplomat.com/2016/04/return-of-asias-quad-natural-us-defense-chief/ (accessed on 22 November 2016).

45 Widmark, Otto, 'India's Aspiration for a Permanent Membership at the Security Council: An Update', *Issue Brief*, Delhi Policy Group, New Delhi, January 2015.

46 Sullivan de Estrada, Kate, 'India and UN Security Council Reform 1990–1997', Unpublished paper (2016).

47 Swart, Lydia, 'Reform of the Security Council: 2007–2013', in *Governing and Managing Change at the United Nations*, vol. 1, (New York: Center for UN Reform Education, September 2013), pp. 23–60.

48 Magalhães Barreto Leite Silva, Marina, 'Spoiler or Reformer? The Uniting for Consensus Group and Security Council Reform', Ph.D. dissertation, Osaka University, January 2014, http://ir.library.osaka-u.ac.jp/dspace/bitstream/11094/34548/1/26639_%E8%AB%96%E6%96%87.pdf (accessed on 20 November 2016).

49 Widmark, 'India's Aspiration for a Permanent Membership at the Security Council', pp. 10–13; Mukherjee, Rohan and David M. Malone, 'India and the UN Security Council: An Ambiguous Tale', *Economic and Political Weekly*, vol. 48, no. 29 (2013), pp. 110–117.

50 Irfan, Hakeem, 'The Mixed Legacy of Defence Minister A. K. Anthony', *Daily News and Analysis*, 12 December 2013, www.dnaindia.com/india/report-the-mixed-legacy-of-defence-minister-ak-antony-1934037 (accessed on 22 February 2015).

51 Ghosh, P. K., 'IONS and the Indian Ocean: Reviving a Listless Initiative', *RSIS Commentaries*, 8 May 2014, www.rsis.edu.sg/wp-content/uploads/2014/07/CO14083.pdf (accessed on 22 February 2015).

52 Neumann, Iver B. and Benjamin de Carvalho, 'Small States and Status', in Benjamin de Carvalho and Iver B. Neumann, eds, *Small State Status Seeking: Norway's Quest for International Standing* (Abingdon and New York: Routledge, 2015).

53 Dormandy, Xenia, 'Is India, or Will It Be, a Responsible Stakeholder?' in Alexander Lennon and Amanda Kozlowski, eds, *Global Powers in the 21st Century* (Cambridge, MA: MIT Press, 2008), pp. 60–76.

54 Lake, David A., 'Great Power Hierarchies and Strategies in Twenty-first Century World Politics', in Walter Carlsnaes, Thomas Risse, and Beth A. Simmons, eds, *Handbook of International Relations*, 2nd edn (London: Sage, 2013), p. 563.

55 Ganguly, Sumit, 'India After Nonalignment: Why Modi Skipped the Summit', *Foreign Affairs*, 19 September 2016, www.foreignaffairs.com/articles/india/2016-09-19/india-after-nonalignment (accessed 6 December 2016).

56 Dixit, J. N., *My South Block Years: Memoirs of a Foreign Secretary* (New Delhi: UBSPD, 1996), p. 377.

57 Ibid., p. 43.

58 Ibid., p. 44.

59 Ibid., p. 378.

60 'Final Document of the Tenth Conference of Heads of State or Government of Non-Aligned Countries, Jakarta, 1–6 September 1992', (UN Doc. A/47/675, 18 November 1992).

61 Sullivan de Estrada, 'India and UN Security Council Reform 1990–1997'.

62 Sullivan de Estrada, Kate and Patrick Quinton-Brown, 'The Myth of India's Non-Aligned Boycott', *The Diplomat* (23 November 2016), http://thediplomat.com/2016/11/the-myth-of-indias-non-aligned-boycott/ (accessed 6 December 2016).

63 Ganguly, 'India After Nonalignment'.

64 Sullivan de Estrada and Quinton-Brown, 'The Myth of India's Non-Aligned Boycott'.

65 Ibid.
66 Efstathopoulos, Charalampos and Dominic Kelly, 'India, Developmental Multilateralism and the Doha Ministerial Conference', *Third World Quarterly*, vol. 35, no. 6 (2014), p. 1066.
67 World Resources Institute, 'Top 10 Emitters in 2012', May 2016, www. wri.org/resources/charts-graphs/top-10-emitters-2012 (accessed on 11 December 2016).
68 Krause, Dan, *It Is Changing After All: India's Stance on 'Responsibility to Protect'*, ORF Occasional Paper no. 90 (New Delhi: Observer Research Foundation, April 2016), p. 2.
69 Hall, Ian, 'Tilting at Windmills? The Indian Debate over the Responsibility to Protect after UNSC Resolution 1973', *Global Responsibility to Protect*, no. 5 (2013), pp. 84–108.
70 Krause, *It is Changing After All*, pp. 32–33.
71 Kumar, A. Vinod, *India and the Nuclear Non-Proliferation Regime: The Perennial Outlier* (Delhi: Cambridge University Press, 2014); Schaffer, Teresita with Joan Rohlfing, *India and the Non-Proliferation System: A Report of the Working Group on an Expanded Non-proliferation System*, Nuclear Threat Initiative, Washington, DC, November 2011, www.nti. org/media/pdfs/IndiaNonProliferationSystem-1111.pdf?_=1326131244 (accessed on 20 November 2016). On India and the Wassenaar Arrangement, see: Rajagopalan, Rajeswari Pillai and Arka Biswas, *Wassenaar Arrangement: The Case of India's Membership*, Observer Research Foundation, New Delhi, May 2016, http://cf.orfonline.org/wp-content/up loads/2016/05/ORF-Occasional-Paper_92.pdf (accessed on 20 November 2016).
72 Chari, P. R., ed., *Indo–US Nuclear Agreement: Seeking Synergy in Bilateralism* (New Delhi: Routledge, 2009); Mistry, Dinshaw, *The US–India Nuclear Agreement: Diplomacy and Domestic Politics* (Delhi: Cambridge University Press, 2014); Sullivan de Estrada and Wheeler, 'Trustworthy Nuclear Sovereigns?'.
73 Sasikumar, Karthika, 'India's Emergence as a Responsible Nuclear Power', *International Journal*, vol. 62, no. 4 (2007), pp. 825–844; Sullivan, Kate, *Is India a Responsible Nuclear Power?* Policy report, S. Rajaratnam School of International Studies, Nanyang Technological University, Singapore, March 2014. For a critical view, see Narlikar, Amrita, 'India Rising: Responsible to Whom?' *International Affairs*, vol. 89, no. 3 (2013), pp. 595–614.
74 Das, Ajaya Kumar, 'India–US Relations: Assessing India's Soft Power', Ph.D. dissertation, Nanyang Technological University, Singapore, 2015, p. 204.
75 United States, White House, Office of the Press Secretary, 'Joint Statement between President George W. Bush and Prime Minister Manmohan Singh', 18 July 2005, http://georgewbushwhitehouse.archives.gov/news/releases/ 2005/07/20050718-6.html (accessed on 21 November 2016).
76 See Das, *India–US Relations*, pp. 220–221, for more acknowledgments by American officials regarding India's 'responsible' behaviour on nuclear proliferation-related issues.
77 The significance of the deal lies in the formal separation of India's civilian and military nuclear facilities, which in effect amounts to acceptance by

NSG members of India's status as a nuclear power even as it remains outside the NPT.

78 Kohli, *The Success of India's Democracy*; Rudolph, Susanne Hoeber and Lloyd I. Rudolph, 'New Dimensions in Indian Democracy', *Journal of Democracy*, vol. 13, no. 1 (2002), pp. 52–66.

79 Singh, Manmohan, 'PM's Valedictory Address to the Fifth Session of the 14th Lok Sabha', 30 August 2005, http://archivepmo.nic.in/drmanmoha nsingh/speech-details.php?nodeid=172 (accessed on 5 December 2016).

80 United States, Department of State, 'Hearing on U.S.–India Civil Nuclear Cooperation Initiative: R. Nicholas Burns, Under Secretary for Political Affairs, Remarks as Prepared for the Senate Foreign Relations Committee', 2 November 2005, https://2001-2009.state.gov/p/us/rm/2005/ 55969.htm (accessed on 21 November 2016).

81 United States Senate, Committee on Environment and Public Works, 'Hearing Statements', 16 June 2006, www.epw.senate.gov/hearing_statem ents.cfm?id=257222 (accessed on 21 November 2016).

82 Blackwill, Robert D., 'A New Deal for New Delhi', *Wall Street Journal*, 21 March 2005, www.wsj.com/articles/SB111136460616084700 (accessed on 21 November 2016).

83 'Remarks of Secretary of State Condoleezza Rice'.

84 Piccone, Ted, *Five Rising Democracies and the Fate of the International Liberal Order* (Washington, DC: Brookings Institution Press, 2016), p. 82.

85 See, for example, Halarnkar, Samar, 'Hindu Republic: India Is Being Recreated into a Majoritarian State', *Hindustan Times*, 20 October 2016, www.hindustantimes.com/columns/india-is-being-gradually-recreated-into-a -majoritarian-state/story-7lqUnXaK6figKo2BFikUeK.html (accessed on 6 Decmber 2016); Jacob, Happymon, 'Rise of the Garrison State', *The Hindu*, 19 October 2016, www.thehindu.com/opinion/lead/happymon-ja cob-on-the-rise-of-the-garrison-state/article9235788.ece (accessed on 6 Decmber 2016); Jha, Prem Shankar, 'Overcome by a Sense of Betrayal', *The Hindu*, 15 January 2013, www.thehindu.com/opinion/lead/overcom e-by-a- sense-of-betrayal/article4307678.ece (accessed on 6 Decmber 2016).

86 Zakaria, Fareed, 'Interview with Narendra Modi; Interview with Bill Clin- ton', *Global Public Square*, broadcast 21 September 2014, http://edition.cnn. com/TRANSCRIPTS/1409/21/fzgps.01.html (accessed on 3 December 2016).

87 Manmohan Singh, cited in: Varshney, Ashutosh, 'Mass Politics or Elite Politics? India's Economic Reforms in Comparative Perspective', *Journal of Policy Reform*, vol. 2, no. 4 (1998), p. 309.

88 World Bank, 'World Bank National Accounts Data, and OECD National Accounts Data Files', http://data.worldbank.org/indicator/NE.TRD. GNFS.ZS?end=2014&start=1991 (accessed on 17 November 2016).

89 Joshi, *Indian Power Projection*.

90 Neumann, Iver B., 'Status Is Cultural: Durkheimian Poles and Weberian Russians Seek Great Power Status', in T. V. Paul, Deborah Welch Larson and William C. Wohlforth, eds, *Status in World Politics* (New York: Cambridge University Press, 2014), p. 86.

91 Mohan, C. Raja, 'Indian Military Diplomacy: Humanitarian Assistance and Disaster Relief', Institute for South Asian Studies, National University of Singapore, Working paper no. 184, 26 March 2014.

92 Mukherjee, Anit, *India as a Net Security Provider: Concept and Impediments* (Singapore: S. Rajaratnam School of International Studies, Nanyang Technological University, August 2014) www.rsis.edu.sg/wp-content/uploads/2014/09/PB_140903_India-Net-Security.pdf (accessed on 21 November 2016).

93 Kifner, John, 'India Decides Not to Send Troops to Iraq Now', *New York Times*, 15 July 2003, www.nytimes.com/2003/07/15/world/after-the-war-other-forces-india-decides-not-to-send-troops-to-iraq-now.html (accessed on 23 February 2015).

94 Destradi, Sandra, 'India and the Civil War in Sri Lanka: On the Failures of Regional Conflict Management in South Asia', Working paper no. 154 (2010), German Institute of Global and Area Studies, www.giga-hamburg.de/en/system/files/publications/wp154_destradi.pdf (accessed on 22 February 2015). That Indian military aid was not insubstantial is shown in: Gokhale, Nitin, *Sri Lanka: From War to Peace* (New Delhi: Har-Anand, 2009).

95 Mohan, C. Raja, 'Debating India's Stand on Military Aid to Afghanistan', *Indian Express*, 7 July 2009, http://archive.indianexpress.com/news/debating-indias-stand-on-military-aid-to-afghanistan/486099/0 (accessed on 22 February 2015); 'Taliban Praise India for Resisting Afghan Entanglement', *Express Tribune*, 17 June 2002, http://tribune.com.pk/story/395024/taliban-praise-india-for-resisting-afghan-entanglement/ (accessed on 22 February 2015); Swami, Praveen, 'Upset with Delay, Kabul Shelves Request for Arms Aid from Delhi', *Indian Express*, 30 October 2014, http://indianexpress.com/article/india/india-others/upset-with-delay-kabul-shelves-request-for-arms-aid-from-delhi/ (accessed on 22 February 2015).

96 Dormandy, Xenia, 'Is India, or Will It Be, a Responsible Stakeholder?' in Alexander Lennon and Amanda Kozlowski, eds, *Global Powers in the 21st Century*, Cambridge (MA: MIT Press, 2008), pp. 60–76.

97 Sullivan, Kate, 'India's Ambivalent Projection of Self as a Global Power: Between Compliance and Resistance', in Kate Sullivan, ed., *Competing Visions of India in World Politics: India's Rise Beyond the West* (Basingstoke: Palgrave Macmillan, 2015), pp. 15–33.

98 Chacko, Priya, *Indian Foreign Policy: The Politics of Postcolonial Identity from 1947 to 2004* (Abingdon and New York: Routledge, 2004); Ganguly, Sumit, *Hindu Nationalism and the Foreign Policy of India's Bharatiya Janata Party* (Washington, DC: Transatlantic Academy, 2015); Ogden, Chris, *Hindu Nationalism and the Evolution of Contemporary Indian Security* (New Delhi: Oxford University Press, 2014).

99 Basrur, 'Modi's Foreign Policy Fundamentals'.

100 Bhatt, Chetan, *Hindu Nationalism: Origins, Ideologies and Myths* (Oxford and New York: Oxford University Press, 2001).

101 Tiwari, Ravish, 'BJP Calls for a Muscular Foreign Policy: Panchamrit to Replace Panchsheel', *India Today*, 4 April 2016, http://indiatoday.intoday.in/story/bjp-foreign-policy-national-executive/1/428383.html (accessed on 20 May 2016).

102 Clunan, Anne, 'Why Status Matters in World Politics', in Paul et al., *Status in World Politics*, p. 283.

103 Neumann and Carvalho, 'Small States and Status', pp. 10–11.

5 Conclusion

The purpose of this short book has been to offer a fresh interpretation of India's search for higher status over the past seven decades. More concretely, it has sought to explore the complexities that characterise the relationship between status and power in the Indian case. The standard realist approach tends to adhere to a simple correlation between the two: low power equals low status and, as power rises, so does status. While status accommodation is deemed to matter, it is generally taken for granted that accommodation is founded on recognition of power and compatibility of interests. Our finding is that the relationship is not simply linear. Without doubt, power is a prerequisite for sustainable high status, but status is also attainable with relatively limited power under certain conditions. We also find that states with or without power can exercise creative options in order to maximise status.

Our study, building on recent literature on status in world politics, and drawing on Milner's study of status relationships to take this literature further, has looked at two components of status-seeking behaviour displayed by states. In the first component are two types of material association: the possession of material attributes that are socially valued, mainly, economic and military power; and proximity to high-status states, which opens up diverse avenues for status enhancement. The second component is normative and centres on the extent to which a state aspiring to higher status conforms to dominant international norms that are themselves more often than not established by powerful high-status states. In the present instance, we examined India's conformity or otherwise to norms in three distinct categories: prevailing norms of interstate interaction that define the international order (basic patterns of strategic politics); the (contested) norm of nuclear non-proliferation; and the norm of liberal democracy, which encompasses adherence to both political and economic freedom of action within states.

Findings

The three empirical chapters in this book studied three distinct periods: the Nehru era (1947–64), the post-Nehru era (1964–1991) and the post-Cold War era (1991–2016). The watershed years are important: 1964 marked the end of what was indubitably the foundational stage of India's internal and external political and economic life under the towering figure of Jawaharlal Nehru; 1991 was a watershed imposed from without: the year when the end of the Cold War and a severe balance-of-payments crisis triggered fundamental changes in India's foreign and domestic policies. The three periods are distinctive in the ways that national policies have been applied with respect to the attainment of status as per the criteria given above.

Under Nehru's leadership, India's material power was limited. As a developing post-colonial society, India possessed potential and resources, but limited capacity to convert them into actual capabilities. Nehru's primary focus was on kick-starting a weak economy and ensuring that the infant nation-state held together politically. Given the enormity of the task, he and his colleagues chose to downplay the need for military power, which remained weak and neglected throughout his premiership. On the second aspect of material associations, Nehru also chose to avoid proximity to the major powers. The consequence of this twin material weakness was that India was unprepared for the 1962 war with China, was roundly defeated in battle, and suffered a severe setback to such status gains as had been made without recourse to power. These gains were not insubstantial. Nehru's India challenged two major collective norms of the day: the ideological-cum-power political norm that divided the world into competing Cold War camps; and the economic norm, established by the United States, which emphasised the legitimacy and utilitarian value of global capitalism. Refusing to accept the prevailing norms, India instead chose to focus on alternative ways to achieve both security and status, and these were represented by the effort to build a 'third force' – which eventually grew into the Non-Aligned Movement (NAM) – and the adoption of a mixed economy with features of both capitalism and socialism. As regards democracy, Nehru's deep commitment to it ensured that the difficult task of creating a democratic polity in a diverse and in many ways unequal society was sustained despite the plethora of challenges facing state formation and societal stability. By crafting an independent and creative strategy, Nehru was able to acquire for India and himself considerable influence and respect. However, these gains were short-lived: the shattering blow of the war with China left the country uncertain of where it stood. The chief lesson was that status is possible with little power, but it is subject to the test of power – a test for which preparation has to be made over time.

In the post-Nehru period, the neglect of power was remedied. Slow economic growth precluded faster change in this respect, but India's military received higher levels of funding and duly emerged with the wherewithal to confront two adversaries, Pakistan and China. India also hedged on nuclear weapons, slowly building technical capability, but not sufficiently enthused to quickly build an arsenal, not even after a single test in 1974 to demonstrate its capability. The embrace of material power, then, was partial. Like Nehru, later prime ministers sought to keep a safe distance from the major powers; and like him, they were forced by political exigency to lean on the dominant powers in times of trouble. The sense that India was becoming strategically isolated by the emergence of a US–China–Pakistan nexus compelled Indira Gandhi to sign the 1971 friendship treaty with the Soviet Union, which compromised her commitment to non-alignment. For lack of viable alternatives, India also became increasingly dependent on Moscow for arms. But the discomfiting necessity of strategic proximity to a major power also brought security, as India now had the confidence that came with the combination of rising power and a protected flank. The nuclear test also underlined its strategic autonomy.

On the normative side, India continued on the trajectory set by Nehru, rejecting both the Cold War and global capitalism and playing a spearhead role in the NAM and the G77. But even as it rejected the global order, it emulated the major powers in its own bailiwick, intervening periodically in its neighbouring states and assuming a policing role in the region around it. While global resistance to the Cold War and the world economy brought status benefits of one kind, local order management brought another. The crossing of the nuclear weapon threshold, however, led to the imposition of non-proliferation pressures without yielding the possible gains that might have accrued from actually becoming a nuclear power. Finally, India's democratic credentials came under a cloud with Indira Gandhi's declaration of a state of emergency after her leadership had been challenged by a court order. On the whole, this was a period that opened up an alternative pathway to status through power, though limited by India's refusal to acquiesce to global norms, but which allowed India to retain a modicum of prestige along existing alternative lines. Whereas Nehru had sought and obtained (short-lived) status through a largely non-materialist and non-conformist approach, his successors were somewhat more successful in acquiring status through a combination of material adaptation and normative rejection.

In the post-Cold War era, India went two steps further. First, it dropped all its earlier inhibitions with regard to the acquisition of material power, including nuclear weapons; began associating with the leading power, the United States, as well as other strategic partners; and opened up to the world economy – a combination that quickly raised its status to that of an 'emerging power.' Second, and this is exceptional, even as its power grew, India became less interventionist and more focused on becoming a net security provider exercising military restraint. Asserting its claim to status as a democracy and a 'responsible' power devoted to the provision of public goods without the use of force, India reversed its own past strategic behaviour (and that of other rising powers in history) to stake a claim to the status of a 'leading power.' The present strategy thus involves closer adherence to the material and normative criteria of status that we have employed in this study, with the additional creative feature of military restraint. The strategy has worked quite well, bringing most notably a change in the rules of nuclear commerce and indirect recognition of India's claims to being a legitimate nuclear power. But it is not without pitfalls, since India has found it difficult to convince other states that it has a right to become a member of the non-proliferation regime. More importantly, post-Cold War India has not as yet faced the kind of power test that Nehru and Rajiv Gandhi failed.

Our study shows variation in the relationship between status and power. Power is not the sole requisite for status, as we know from the difficulties faced by China, Pakistan and Russia – all of which are hamstrung by their differences with US-led global norms. On the other hand, as the Indian experience under Nehru demonstrates, a fair degree of status may be achieved without power or even acquiescence to international norms, though it is always subject to the power test. A combination of material power and adherence to norms is the strongest basis for achieving higher status. And if norm creation is added on – assuming it is sustainable – there is an additional basis for attaining high status.

Contributions of the study

Our study, we believe, makes significant contributions to policy making and scholarship. First, it helps to grasp the complexities of Indian foreign policy by disentangling security-seeking behaviour and status-seeking behaviour. In particular, it helps to explain some aspects of strategic policy that appear to be puzzling – for example, why India's conventional and nuclear military acquisitions do not seem to fit well with strategy;[1] or why India invests inordinate diplomatic energy and capital on membership of the Nuclear Suppliers Group when it has little bearing on national security. In both cases, the answer is that these phenomena represent status-seeking behaviour, which is an important dimension of foreign policy. Second, the analysis in these pages can be applied to other states to tease out the complexities of the security-seeking and status-seeking policies they adopt. A comparative study of status seeking could well be a productive line of inquiry that brings deeper insights. And third, this book paves the way for more careful theorising on the power–status relationship. While we have given equal value to material power and norms, it may be worth debating their relative ranking and whether this varies in different cases.

Note

1 We recognise that there may be other explanations as well, for instance vested interests, but believe that status seeking has to be taken into account as a potential factor and does offer considerable explanatory value.

Bibliography

'About Social Capital', Kennedy School of Government, Harvard University, n.d., www.hks.harvard.edu/programs/saguaro/about-social-capital (accessed on 22 February 2015).

Abraham, Itty, 'From Bandung to NAM: Non-Alignment and Indian Foreign Policy, 1947–65', *Commonwealth and Comparative Politics*, vol. 46, no. 2 (2008), pp.195–219.

Alden, Chris, Sally Morphet and Marco Antonio Vieira, *The South in World Politics* (Basingstoke: Palgrave Macmillan, 2010).

Anthony, Denise L. and John L. Campbell, 'States, Social Capital and Cooperation: Looking Back on Governing the Commons', *International Journal of the Commons*, vol. 5, no. 2 (2011) pp. 284–302 (accessed on 22 February 2015).

Arnold, Guy, *Historical Dictionary of the Non-Aligned and Third World* (Lanham, MD: Scarecrow Press, 2006).

Arora, K. C., *V. K. Krishna Menon: A Biography* (New Delhi: Sanchar Publishing House, 1998).

Bajpai, Kanti, Saira Basit and V. Krishnappa, eds, *India's Grand Strategy: History, Theory, Cases* (New Delhi/Abingdon: Routledge, 2014).

Bajpai, G. S., 'India and the Balance of Power', *Indian Yearbook of International Affairs*, vol. 1 (1952), pp. 1–8.

Banerji, Devika and Rishi Shah, 'India Overtakes Japan to Become Third-Largest Economy in Purchasing Power Parity', *Economic Times*, April 9, 2012, http://articles.economictimes.indiatimes.com/2012-04-19/news/31367838_1_ppp-terms-india-s-gdp-power-parity (accessed on July 6, 2012).

Baru, Sanjaya, *Strategic Consequences of India's Economic Performance* (New Delhi: Academic Foundation, 2006).

Baru, Sanjaya, *The Accidental Prime Minister: The Making and Unmaking of Manmohan Singh* (New Delhi: Viking, 2014).

Basrur, Rajesh, 'Modi's Foreign Policy Fundamentals: A Trajectory Unchanged', *International Affairs*, vol. 93, no. 1 (2017), pp. 7–26.

Basrur, Rajesh M., *India's External Relations: A Theoretical Analysis* (New Delhi: Commonwealth Publishers, 2000).

Basrur, Rajesh M., *Minimum Deterrence and India's Nuclear Security* (Stanford, CA: Stanford University Press, 2006).

Basrur, Rajesh, 'India: A Major Power in the Making', in Thomas J. Volgy, Renato Corbetta, Keith A. Grant and Ryan G. Baird, eds, *Major Powers and the Quest for Status in International Politics: Global and Regional Perspectives* (New York: Palgrave, 2011), pp. 181–202.

Bellon, Bertrand and George Niosi, *The Decline of the American Economy*, trans. Robert Chodos and Ellen Garmaise (Montreal and New York: Black Rose Books, 1989).

Bhagwati, Jagdish N. and T. N. Srinivasan, *Foreign Trade Regimes and Economic Development: India* (Cambridge, MA: National Bureau of Economic Research, 1975).

Bhatt, Chetan, *Hindu Nationalism: Origins, Ideologies and Myths* (Oxford and New York: Oxford University Press, 2001).

Bhattacharya, A. K., 'Two Months That Changed India', *Business Standard*, 2 July 2011, www.business-standard.com/article/beyond-business/two-months-that-changed-india-111070200041_1.html (accessed on 18 November 2016).

Blackwill, Robert D., 'A New Deal for New Delhi', *Wall Street Journal*, 21 March 2005, www.wsj.com/articles/SB111136460616084700 (accessed on 21 November 2016).

Blank, Stephen, 'The Geostrategic Implications of the Indo-American Strategic Partnership', *India Review*, vol. 6, no. 1 (2007), pp. 1–24.

Boquerat, Gilles, *No Strings Attached? India's Policies and Foreign Aid, 1947–1966* (New Delhi: Manohar, 2003).

Bowles, Chester, 'America and Russia in India', *Foreign Affairs*, vol. 49 (July 1971), pp. 636–651.

Brands, H. W., *India and the United States: The Cold Peace* (Boston: Twayne Publishers, 1990).

Brecher, Michael, 'Non-alignment Under Stress: The West and the India-China Border War', *Pacific Affairs*, vol. 52, no. 4 (Winter 1979–1980), pp. 612–630.

Brecher, Michael, *Nehru: A Political Biography (Abridged Edition)* (Boston: Beacon Press, 1959).

Brennan, Geoffrey and Philip Pettit, *The Economy of Esteem* (Oxford: Oxford University Press, 2004).

Brewster, David, *India's Ocean: The Story of India's Bid for Regional Leadership* (Abingdon: Routledge, 2014).

Brittingham, Michael Alan, 'China's Contested Rise: Sino–U.S. Relations and the Social Construction of Great Power Status', in Sujian Guo and Shiping Hua, eds, *New Dimensions of Chinese Foreign Policy* (Lanham MD and Plymouth: Lexington Books, 2007), pp. 83–108.

Bromley, Simon, *American Power and the Prospects for International Order* (Cambridge: Polity Press, 2008).

Brown, Judith M., *Nehru: A Political Life* (New Haven, CT: Yale University Press, 2003).

Brown, Judith M., *Modern India: The Origins of an Asian Democracy* (Oxford: Oxford University Press, 1994).

Bukovansky, Mlada, Ian Clark, Robyn Eckersley, Richard Price, Christian Reus-Smit and Nicholas J. Wheeler, *Special Responsibilities: Global Problems and American Power* (Cambridge: Cambridge University Press, 2012).

Bull, Hedley, *The Anarchical Society: A Study of Order in World Politics*, 3rd edn (Basingstoke: Palgrave, 2002).

Bull, Hedley and Adam Watson, eds, *The Expansion of International Society* (Oxford: Clarendon Press, 1984).

Burawoy, Michael, 'The Extended Case Method', in Michael Burawoy, ed., *Ethnography Unbound: Power and Resistance in the Modern Metropolis* (Berkeley: University of California Press), pp. 271–287.

Busby, Joshua W., 'Good States: Prestige and Reputational Concerns of Major Powers under Unipolarity', Paper presented to the Annual Meeting of the American Political Science Association, Washington DC, 1–4 December 2005.

Buzan, Barry, 'From International System to International Society: Structural Realism and Regime Theory Meet the English School', *International Organization*, vol. 47, no. 3 (1993), pp. 327–352.

Buzan, Barry, *The United States and the Great Powers: World Politics in the Twenty-First Century* (Malden MA and Cambridge: Polity Press, 2004).

Chacko, Priya, *Indian Foreign Policy: The Politics of Postcolonial Identity from 1947 to 2004* (Abingdon and New York: Routledge, 2004).

Chagla, M. C., *Roses in December: An Autobiography* (Bombay: Bharatiya Vidya Bhavan, 1974).

Chari, P. R., '"Indo–Soviet Military Cooperation": A Review', *Asian Survey*, vol. XIX, no. 3 (March 1979), pp. 230–244.

Chari, P. R., ed., *Indo–US Nuclear Agreement: Seeking Synergy in Bilateralism* (New Delhi: Routledge, 2009).

Chaudhuri, Rudra, *Forged in Crisis: India and the United States since 1947* (London: Hurst, 2014).

Chellaney, Brahma, *Nuclear Proliferation: The U.S.–Indian Conflict* (New Delhi: Orient Longman, 1993).

Chengappa, Raj, *Weapons of Peace* (New Delhi: HarperCollins, 2000).

Chopra, Pran, 'India: Regional Supercop?' *Express Magazine* (21 May 1989), p. 1.

Clunan, Anne L., 'Why Status Matters in World Politics', in T. V. Paul, Deborah Welch Larson and William C. Wohlforth, eds, *Status in World Politics* (New York: Cambridge University Press, 2014), pp. 273–296.

Cohen, Stephen P. and Sunil Dasgupta, *Arming without Aiming: India's Military Modernization* (Washington, D.C.: Brookings Institution Press, 2010).

Cohen, Stephen P., *India: Emerging Power* (Washington, DC: Brookings Institution Press, 2001).

Copley, Gregory, 'Inevitable India, Inevitable Power', *Defense and Foreign Affairs*, vol. XVI, no. 12 (December 1988), pp. 6–9, 28–29, 52.

Constituent Assembly (Legislative) Debates (Internet Edition), vol. 17, 25 November 1948, http://parliamentofindia.nic.in/ls/debates/vol7p13.htm (accessed on 15 August 2016).

Constituent Assembly (Legislative) Debates (Internet Edition), vol. V, pp. 3315–3334.

Cooper, Andrew F., Richard A. Higgott and Kim Richard Nossal, *Relocating Middle Powers: Australia and Canada in a Changing World Order* (Vancouver, BC: University of British Columbia Press, 1993).

Cooper, Richard, 'Economic Interdependence and Foreign Policy in the Seventies', *World Politics*, vol. 24, no. 2 (January 1972).

Corbridge, Stuart and John Harriss, *Reinventing India: Liberalization, Hindu Nationalism and Popular Democracy* (Cambridge: Polity, 2000).

Curtis, Lisa, 'India's Expanding Role in Asia: Adapting to Rising Power Status', *Backgrounder*, no. 2008, Heritage Foundation, 20 February 2007.

Daase, Christopher, Caroline Fehl, Anna Geis and Georgias Kalliarakis, eds, *Recognition in International Relations: Rethinking a Political Concept in a Global Context* (Basingstoke and New York: Palgrave Macmillan, 2015).

Das, Ajaya Kumar, 'India–US Relations: Assessing India's Soft Power', Ph.D. dissertation, Nanyang Technological University, Singapore, 2015.

Datta-Ray, Sunanda K., 'Region's New Bogey?' *Statesman* (5 March 1989), reprinted in *Indian Ocean Review*, vol. 2, no. 2 (June 1989), p. I.

Dayal, Rajeshwar, *A Life of Our Times* (London: Sangam, 1998).

de Carvalho, Benjamin and Jon Harald Sande Lie, 'Small States and Status Seeking: Norway's Quest for Higher Standing', in Benjamin de Carvalho and Iver B. Neumann, eds, *A Great Power Performance: Norway's Quest for Higher Standing* (Abingdon and New York: Routledge, 2015), pp. 56–72.

de Lange, Deborah E., *Power and Influence: The Embeddedness of Nations* (New York: Palgrave Macmillan, 2010).

Deng, Yong, *China's Struggle for Status: The Realignment of International Relations* (New York: Cambridge University Press, 2008).

Destradi, Sandra, 'India and the Civil War in Sri Lanka: On the Failures of Regional Conflict Management in South Asia', Working paper 154 (2010), German Institute of Global and Area Studies, www.giga-hamburg.de/en/system/files/publications/wp154_destradi.pdf (accessed on 22 February 2015).

Dimitrov, Radoslav S., 'The Paris Agreement on Climate Change: Behind Closed Doors', *Global Environmental Politics*, vol. 16, no. 3 (August 2016), pp. 1–11.

Dominguez, Silvia and Celeste Watkins, 'Creating Networks for Survival and Mobility: Social Capital Among African-American and Latin-American Low-income Mothers', *Social Problems*, vol. 50, no. 1 (2003), pp. 111–135.

Dormandy, Xenia, 'Is India, or Will It Be, a Responsible Stakeholder?' in T. J. Lennon Alexander and Amanda Kozlowski, eds, *Global Powers in the 21st Century*, (Cambridge, MA: MIT Press, 2008), pp. 60–76.

Efstathopoulos, Charalampos, 'Leadership in the WTO: Brazil, India and the Doha Development Agenda', *Cambridge Review of International Affairs*, vol. 25, no. 2 (2012), pp. 269–293.

Efstathopoulos, Charalampos and Dominic Kelly, 'India, Developmental Multilateralism and the Doha Ministerial Conference', *Third World Quarterly*, vol. 35, no. 6 (2014), pp. 1066–1081.

Elliott, Lorraine, *The Global Politics of the Environment*, 2nd edn (New York: New York University Press, 2004).

Erickson, Andrew S., Walter C. Ladwig III and Justin D. Mikolay, 'Diego Garcia and the United States' Emerging Indian Ocean Strategy', *Asian Security*, vol. 6, no. 3 (2010), pp. 214–237.

Evans, Gareth, 'Foreign Policy and Good International Citizenship', Address by the Minister for Foreign Affairs, Senator Gareth Evans, Canberra, 6 March 1990', www.gevans.org/speeches/old/1990/060390_fm_fpandgoo dinternationalcitizen.pdf (accessed on 26 November 2016).

'Final Document of the Tenth Conference of Heads of State or Government of Non-Aligned Countries, Jakarta, 1–6 September 1992' (*UN Doc.* A/47/675, 18 November 1992).

Fordham, Benjamin O., 'Who Wants to Be a Major Power? Explaining the Expansion of Foreign Policy Ambition', *Journal of Peace Research*, vol. 48, no. 5 (2011), pp. 587–603.

Foster, John Bellamy, *The Ecological Revolution: Making Peace with the Planet* (New York: Monthly Review Press, 2009).

Frankel, Francine R., 'Preface', in Francine R. Frankel, ed., *Bridging the Non-Proliferation Divide: The United States and India* (Delhi: Konark, 1995), pp. v–x.

Fuchs, Andreas and Krishna Chaitanya Vadlamannati, 'The Needy Donor: An Empirical Analysis of India's Aid Motives', *World Development*, vol. 44 (2013), pp. 110–128.

Fukuyama, Francis, *The End of History and the Last Man* (New York: Free Press, 1992).

Gandhi, Indira, 'Preface', in Planning Commission, *4th Five-Year Plan* (New Delhi: Government of India, 1970), http://planningcommission.nic.in/pla ns/planrel/fiveyr/4th/4ppre.htm (accessed on 2 December 2016).

Gandhi, Indira, 'Address of Shrimati Indira Gandhi, Prime Minister of India: The Unfinished Revolution', Part V of 'A Special Report: What Happened at Stockholm', *Bulletin of the Atomic Scientists*, vol. XXVIII, no. 7 (September 1972), pp. 35–38.

Gandhi, Indira, 'India's Foreign Policy', *Foreign Affairs*, vol. 51, no. 65 (1972), pp. 65–77.

Ganguly, Rajat, 'Indian Military Transformation in the Twenty First Century', in Pauline Eadie and Wyn Rees, eds, *The Evolution of Military Power in the West and Asia: Security Policy in the Post-Cold War Era* (Abingdon and New York: Routledge, 2016), pp. 167–188.

Ganguly, Sumit, 'India's Pathway to Pokhran II: The Prospects and Sources of New Delhi's Nuclear Weapons Program', *International Security*, vol. 23, no. 4 (1999), pp. 148–177.

Ganguly, Sumit, 'Think Again: India's Rise', *Foreign Policy* (5 July 2012).

Ganguly, Sumit, *Hindu Nationalism and the Foreign Policy of India's Bharatiya Janata Party* (Washington, DC: Transatlantic Academy, 2015).

Ganguly, Sumit, 'India After Nonalignment: Why Modi Skipped the Summit', *Foreign Affairs*, 19 September 2016, https://www.foreignaffairs.com/articles/india/2016-09-19/india-after-nonalignment (accessed on 6 December 2016).

Ganguly, Sumit and Rahul Mukherji, *India Since 1980* (Cambridge: Cambridge University Press, 2011).

Gerring, John, 'What Is a Case Study and What Is It Good for?' *American Political Science Review*, vol. 98, no. 2 (May 2004), pp. 341–354.

Ghose, Arundhati, 'Negotiating the CTBT: India's Security Concerns and Nuclear Disarmament', *Journal of International Affairs*, vol. 51, no. 1 (1997), pp. 239–261.

Ghosh, P. K., 'IONS and the Indian Ocean: Reviving a Listless Initiative', *RSIS Commentaries*, 8 May 2014, www.rsis.edu.sg/wp-content/uploads/2014/07/CO14083.pdf (accessed on 22 February 2015).

Gilpin, Robert, *War and Change in World Politics* (New York: Cambridge University Press, 1981).

Goertz Lall, Betty, 'Notes from Asia and Germany', *Bulletin of the Atomic Scientists* (November 1965).

Gokhale, Nitin, *Sri Lanka: From War to Peace* (New Delhi: Har-Anand, 2009).

Gopal, Sarvepalli, *Jawaharlal Nehru: A Biography (Abridged Edition)* (New Delhi: Oxford University Press, 1989).

Gordon, Sandy, *India's Rise as an Asian Power: Nation, Neighbourhood, and Region* (Washington, DC: Georgetown University Press, 2014).

Gupta, Sisir, *India and the International System* (New Delhi: Vikas, 1981).

Gupte, Pranay, *Mother India: A Political Biography of Indira Gandhi* (New York: Macmillan, 1992).

Halarnkar, Samar, 'Hindu Republic: India Is Being Recreated into a Majoritarian State', *Hindustan Times*, 20 October 2016, www.hindustantimes.com/columns/india-is-being-gradually-recreated-into-a-majoritarian-state/story-7lqUnXaK6figKo2BFikUeK.html (accessed on 6 December 2016).

Hall, Ian, 'Tilting at Windmills? The Indian Debate over the Responsibility to Protect after UNSC Resolution 1973', *Global Responsibility to Protect, no. 5* (2013), pp. 84–108.

Hall, Ian, ed., *The Engagement of India: Strategies and Responses* (Washington, DC: Georgetown University Press, 2014).

Hardgrave, Robert L. and Stanley A. Kochanek, *India: Government and Politics in a Developing Nation (Sixth Edition)* (Orlando, FL: Harcourt Brace & Co., 2000).

Harrison, Selig, *India: The Most Dangerous Decades* (Princeton, NJ: Princeton University Press, 1960).

Harrison, Selig, 'Troubled India and Her Neighbours', *Foreign Affairs*, vol. 43, no. 2 (January 1965) https://www.foreignaffairs.com/articles/asia/1965-01-01/troubled-india-and-her-neighbors (accessed on 6 December 2016).

Harrison, Selig S., 'The Forgotten Bargain', *World Policy Journal* (Fall 2006), pp. 1–13.

Harshe, Rajen, 'India's Nonalignment: An Attempt at Conceptual Reconstruction', *Economic and Political Weekly* (17–24 February 1990), pp. 399–405.

Hassler, Sabine, *Reforming the UN Security Council Membership* (Abingdon and New York: Routledge, 2014).

Haynes, Michael, 'Counting Soviet Deaths in the Great Patriotic War: A Note', *Europe-Asia Studies*, vol. 55, no. 2 (2003), pp. 303–309.

Hess, Natalie M., 'EU Relations with "Emerging" Strategic Partners: Brazil, India and South Africa', *Focus*, no. 2 (2012) www.giga-hamburg.de/en/publication/eu-relations-with-emerging-strategic-partners-brazil-india-and-south-africa (accessed on 10 February 2015).

Hoge Jr, James F., 'A Global Power Shift in the Making: Is the United States Ready?' *Foreign Affairs*, vol. 83, no. 4 (July-August 2004), pp. 2–7.

'India: Indira Gandhi's Dictatorship Digs In', *Time Magazine*, 14 July 1975, http://content.time.com/time/magazine/article/0,9171,917627,00.html (accessed on 28 November 2016).

'India deserves UNSC Permanent Membership, Says PM Narendra Modi', *Economic Times* (8 June 2015) http://economictimes.indiatimes.com/article show/47578554.cms?utm_source=contentofinterest&utm_medium=text&utm_campaign=cppst (accessed on 22 July 2016).

India, Ministry of External Affairs, *Annual Report 2015–16*, Appendix XVI, p. 347, https://mea.gov.in/Uploads/PublicationDocs/26525_26525_External_Affairs_English_AR_2015-16_Final_compressed.pdf (accessed on 18 November 2016).

International Commission on Intervention and State Sovereignty, *The Responsibility to Protect: Report of the International Commission on Intervention and State Sovereignty*, Ottawa: International Development Research Centre, December 2001.

International Institute for Strategic Studies, *The Military Balance 2016* (Oxford: Oxford University Press, 2016).

International Institute for Strategic Studies, *The Military Balance 1992–1993* (London: Brassey's, 1992).

Irfan, Hakeem, 'The Mixed Legacy of Defence Minister A.K. Anthony', *Daily News and Analysis*, 12 December 2013, www.dnaindia.com/india/report-the-mixed-legacy-of-defence-minister-ak-antony-1934037 (accessed on 22 February 2015).

Jacob, Happymon, 'Rise of the Garrison State', *The Hindu*, 19 October 2016, www.thehindu.com/opinion/lead/happymon-jacob-on-the-rise-of-the-garrison-state/ article9235788.ece (accessed 6 December 2016).

Jacobsen, Sally, 'A Call to Environmental Order', Part II of 'A Special Report: What Happened at Stockholm', *Bulletin of the Atomic Scientists*, vol. XXVIII, no. 7 (September 1972), pp. 21–25.

Jain, Jagdish P., *India and Disarmament* (New Delhi: Radiant, 1974).

Jaishankar, S., 'India, the United States and China', Fullerton Lecture, International Institute of Strategic Studies, Singapore, 20 July 2015, www.iiss.org/en/events/events/archive/2015-f463/july-636f/fullerton-lecture-jaishankar-f64e (accessed on 10 January 2016).

Jha, Chandra Shekhar, *From Bandung to Tashkent: Glimpses of India's foreign policy* (Delhi: Sangam Books, 1983).

Jha, Prem Shankar, 'Overcome by a Sense of Betrayal', *The Hindu*, 15 January 2013, www.thehindu.com/opinion/lead/overcome-by-a-sense-of-betrayal/article4307678.ece (accessed on 6 December 2016).

Ji, Xianbai, Pradumna Bickram Rana, Wai-Mun Chia and Changtai Li, 'Economic and Strategic Dimensions of Mega-FTAs: A Perception Survey of Asian Opinion Leaders', Working paper, S. Rajaratnam School of International Studies, Nanyang Technological University, Singapore, 9 December 2016.

Joshi, Shashank, *Indian Power Projection: Ambition, Arms and Influence*. Whitehall Papers (London: Royal United Services Institute for Defence and Security Studies, 2015).

Kahler, Miles, *Networked Politics: Agency, Power and Governance* (Ithaca, NY: Cornell University Press, 2009).

Karunakaran, K. P., *India in World Affairs: August 1947–January 1950* (Calcutta: Oxford University Press, 1952).

Keenleyside, T. A., 'The Inception of Indian Foreign Policy: The Non-Nehru Contribution', *South Asia: Journal of South Asian Studies*, vol. 4, no. 2 (1981), pp. 63–78.

Keenleyside, T. A., 'Prelude to Power: The Meaning of Non-Alignment Before Indian Independence', *Pacific Affairs*, vol. 53, no. 3 (1980), pp. 461–483.

Kennedy, Paul, *The Rise and Fall of the Great Powers: Economic Change and Military Conflict from 1500 to 2000* (New York: Random House, 1987).

Keohane, Robert O., 'The Economy of Esteem and Climate Change', *St. Anthony's International Review*, vol. 5, no. 2 (2010), pp. 16–28.

Khan, Mohammed Ayub, 'The Pakistan–American Alliance: Stresses and Strains', *Foreign Affairs*, vol. 42, no. 2 (1964) https://www.foreignaffairs.com/articles/asia/1964-01-01/pakistan-american-alliance (accessed 6 December 2016).

Khilnani, Sunil, Rajiv Kumar, Pratap Bhanu Mehta, Prakash Menon, Nandan Nilekani, Srinath Raghavan, Shyam Saran and Siddharth Varadarajan, *Nonalignment 2.0: A Foreign and Strategic Policy for India in the 21st Century* (Cybercity: Penguin, 2013).

Kifner, John, 'India Decides Not To Send Troops to Iraq Now', *New York Times*, 15 July 2003, www.nytimes.com/2003/07/15/world/after-the-war-other-forces-india-decides-not-to-send-troops-to-iraq-now.html (accessed on 23 February 2015).

Klieman, Aaron S., 'Indira's India: Democracy and Crisis Government', *Political Science Quarterly*, vol. 96, no. 2 (Summer 1981), pp. 241–259.

Klemann, Hein A. M. and Sergei Kudryashov, *Occupied Economies: An Economic History of Nazi-Occupied Europe, 1939–1945* (London: Berg, 2012).

Kochanek, S. A., 'India's Changing Role in the United Nations', *Pacific Affairs*, vol. 53, no. 1 (1980), pp. 48–68.

Kohli, Atul, 'Politics of Economic Liberalization in India', *World Development*, vol. 17, no. 3 (1989), pp. 305–328.

Kohli, Atul, ed., *The Success of India's Democracy* (Cambridge: Cambridge University Press, 2001).

Koshy, Ninan, *Under the Empire: India's New Foreign Policy* (New Delhi: LeftWord Books, 2006).

Kothari, D. S., *Nuclear Explosions and Their Effects* (Delhi: Ministry of Information and Broadcasting, Government of India, 1956).

Krasner, Stephen D., *Structural Conflict: The Third World Against Global Liberalism* (Berkeley: University of California Press, 1985).

Krause, Dan, *It Is Changing After All: India's Stance on 'Responsibility to Protect'*, ORF Occasional paper #90 (New Delhi: Observer Research Foundation, April 2016).

Krishna, Gopal, 'India and the International Order: Retreat from Idealism', in Hedley Bull and Adam Watson, eds, *The Expansion of International Society* (Oxford: Clarendon Press, 1984), pp. 269–288.

Kristensen, Hans M. and Robert S. Norris, 'Global Nuclear Weapons Inventories, 1945–2013', *Bulletin of the Atomic Scientists*, vol. 69, no. 5 (2013), pp. 75–81.

Kristensen, Hans M. and Robert S. Norris, 'Indian Nuclear Forces, 2015', *Bulletin of the Atomic Scientists*, vol. 71, no. 5 (2015) pp. 77–83.

Kumar, Satish, S. D. Pradhan, Kanwal Sibal, Rahul Bedi and Bidisha Ganguly, *India's Strategic Partners: A Comparative Assessment*, New Delhi: Foundation for National Security Research, November 2011, http://fnsr.org/files/Indias_Strategic.pdf (accessed on 10 February 2015).

Kumar, A. Vinod, *India and the Nuclear Non-Proliferation Regime: The Perennial Outlier* (Delhi: Cambridge University Press, 2014).

Lake, David A., 'Great Power Hierarchies and Strategies in Twenty-first Century World Politics', in Walter Carlsnaes, Thomas Risse and Beth A. Simmons, eds, *Handbook of International Relations*, 2nd edn (London: Sage, 2013), pp. 555–577.

Lall, Arthur S., *The Emergence of Modern India* (New York: Columbia University Press, 1981).

Lall, Arthur S., *Negotiating Disarmament: The Eighteen Nation Disarmament Conference*, (Ithaca, NY: Centre for International Studies, 1964).

Larson, Deborah Welch, T. V. Paul and William C. Wohlforth, 'Status and World Order', in T. V. Paul, Deborah Welch Larson and William C. Wohlforth, eds, *Status in World Politics* (New York: Cambridge University Press, 2014), pp. 3–29.

Larson, Deborah Welch and Alexei Shevchenko, 'Status Seekers: Chinese and Russian Responses to U.S. Primacy', *International Security*, vol. 34, no. 4 (2010), pp.63–95.

Larson, Deborah Welch and Alexei Shevchenko, 'Status, Identity and Rising Powers', Working paper #32 (25 October 2010), Montreal: Centre for

International Peace and Security Studies, University of Montreal and McGill University.

Lebow, Richard Ned, *A Cultural Theory of International Relations* (Cambridge: Cambridge University Press, 2008).

Lebow, Richard Ned, 'Fear, Interest and Honour: Outlines of a Theory of International Relations', *International Affairs*, vol. 82, no. 3 (2006), pp. 431–448.

LeoGrande, William M., 'Evolution of the Nonaligned Movement', *Problems of Communism* (January–February 1980), pp. 35–52.

Lobell, Steven E., Norrin M. Ripsman and Jeffrey W. Taliaferro, eds, *Neoclassical Realism, the State, and Foreign Policy* (New York: Cambridge University Press, 2009).

Loke, Beverley, 'Unpacking the Politics of Great Power Responsibility: Nationalist and Maoist China in International Order-building', *European Journal of International Relations*, vol. 22, no. 4 (December 2016), pp. 847–871.

Luce, Edward, *In Spite of the Gods: The Strange Rise of Modern India* (London: Abacus, 2007).

Lundestad, Geir, *East, West, North, South: Major Developments in International Relations Since 1945*. 5th edn (London: Sage, 2005).

M., B., 'Toeing the G-7 Line', *Economic and Political Weekly* (18 February 1989), pp. 343–344.

Malone, David M., *Does the Elephant Dance? Contemporary Indian Foreign Policy* (Oxford: Oxford University Press, 2011).

Mansergh, Nicholas, 'Review: India in World Affairs', *International Affairs*, vol. 29, no. 4 (1953), pp. 524–525.

Mansingh, Surjit, *India's Search for Power* (New Delhi: Sage, 1984).

Maoz, Zeev, *Networks and Nations: The Evolution, Structure and Impact of International Networks, 1816–2001* (Cambridge: Cambridge University Press, 2011).

Mastny, Vojtech, 'The Soviet Union's Partnership with India', *Journal of Cold War Studies*, vol. 12, no. 3 (Summer 2010), pp. 50–90.

Mathur, Colette, Frank-Jürgen Richter and Tarun Das, eds, *India Rising: Emergence of a New World Power* (Singapore: Marshall Cavendish, 2005).

Maxwell, Neville, 'Settlements and Disputes: China's Approach to Territorial Issues', *Economic and Political Weekly* (9 September 2006), pp. 3873–3881.

McCann, Gerard, 'From Diaspora to Third Worldism and the United Nations: India and the Politics of Decolonizing Africa', *Past and Present*, vol. 218, suppl. 8 (2013), pp. 258–280.

McCartney, Matthew, *India: The Political Economy of Growth, Stagnation, and the State, 1951–2007* (Abingdon and New York: Routledge, 2009).

McMahon, Robert J., 'Food as a Diplomatic Weapon: The India Wheat Loan of 1951', *Pacific Historical Review*, vol. 56, no. 3 (1987), pp. 349–377.

Mehta, Pratap Bhanu, 'Still Under Nehru's Shadow? The Absence of Foreign Policy Frameworks in India', *India Review*, vol. 8, no. 3 (2009), pp. 209–233.

Merrill, Dennis, *Bread and the Ballot* (Chapel Hill: University of North Carolina Press, 1990).

Merrill, Dennis, 'Indo-American Relations, 1947–50: A Missed Opportunity in Asia', *Diplomatic History*, vol. 11, no. 3 (1987), pp. 203–226.

Miller, Manjari Chatterjee, 'The Un-Argumentative Indian?: Ideas about the Rise of India and Their Interaction with Domestic Structures', *India Review*, vol. 13, no. 1 (2014), pp. 1–14.

Milner Jr, Murray, *Status and Sacredness: A General Theory of Status Relations and an Analysis of Indian Culture* (New York: Oxford University Press, 1994).

Ministry of External Affairs, *Report of the Committee on the Indian Foreign Service* (Delhi: Ministry of External Affairs, 1966).

Mirichandani, G. G., *India's Nuclear Dilemma* (New Delhi: Popular Book Services, 1968).

Mistry, Dinshaw, *The US–India Nuclear Agreement: Diplomacy and Domestic Politics* (Delhi: Cambridge University Press, 2014).

'Modi: India Can Rise Again', *The Hindu*, 22 September 2014, www.thehindu.com/news/national/modi-india-can-rise-again-as-global-power/article6432851.ece (accessed on 22 September 2014).

Mohan, C. Raja, *Crossing the Rubicon: The Shaping of India's New Foreign Policy* (New York: Palgrave Macmillan, 2003).

Mohan, C. Raja, 'Debating India's Stand on Military Aid to Afghanistan', *Indian Express*, 7 July 2009, http://archive.indianexpress.com/news/debating-indias-stand-on-military-aid-to-afghanistan/486099/0 (accessed on 22 February 2015).

Mohan, C. Raja, 'Indian Military Diplomacy: Humanitarian Assistance and Disaster Relief', Working paper #184, Singapore: Institute for South Asian Studies, National University of Singapore, 26 March 2014.

Morgenthau, Hans J., *Politics Among Nations: The Struggle for Power and Peace*, 4th edn (New York: Alfred A. Knopf, 1967).

Mukherjee, Anit, *India as a Net Security Provider: Concept and Impediments* (Singapore: S. Rajaratnam School of International Studies, Nanyang Technological University, August 2014), https://www.rsis.edu.sg/wp-content/uploads/2014/09/PB_140903_India-Net-Security.pdf (accessed on 21 November 2016).

Mukherjee, Rohan and David M. Malone, 'India and the UN Security Council: An Ambiguous Tale', *Economic and Political Weekly*, vol. 48, no. 29 (2013), pp. 110–117.

Mukherjee, Rohan, 'Statuspolitik as Foreign Policy: Strategic Culture and India's Nuclear Behavior', Paper presented at the workshop on 'The Impact of National Cultures on Foreign Policy Making in a Multipolar World', Berlin, October 3–4, 2014.

Mukherji, Rahul, *Globalization and Deregulation: Ideas, Interests and Institutional Change* (New Delhi: Oxford University Press, 2014).

Munro, Ross H., 'Superpower Rising', *Time* (3 April 1989), pp. 6–13.

Myrdal, Alva, *The Game of Disarmament: How the United States and Russia Run the Arms Race* (New York: Pantheon Books, 1976).

Nadkarni, Vidya, *Strategic Partnerships in Asia: Balancing without Alliances* (Abingdon and New York: Routledge, 2010).

Nagao, Satoru, 'Japan, the United States, and India as Key Balancers in Asia', Working paper, Center for Strategic and International Studies, Washington, DChttps://www.csis.org/programs/japan-chair/strategic-japan-working-papers (accessed on 22 November 2016).

Nageswaran, V. Anantha and Gulzar Natarajan, *Can India Grow? Challenges, Opportunities and the Way Forward* (Washington, DC: Carnegie Endowment for International Peace, 2016).

Nandy, Ashis, 'Between Two Gandhis: Psychopolitical Aspects of the Nuclear-ization of India', *Asian Survey*, vol. 14, no. 11 (November 1974), pp. 966–970.

Naoroji, Dadabhai, *Poverty and un-British Rule in India* (London: Swan Sonnenschein, 1901).

Narang, Vipin, 'Five Myths about India's Nuclear Posture', *Washington Quarterly*, vol. 36, no. 3 (2013), pp. 143–157.

Narlikar, Amrita, 'Peculiar Chauvinism or Strategic Calculation? Explaining the Negotiating Strategy of a Rising India', *International Affairs*, vol. 82, no. 1 (2006), pp. 58–76.

Narlikar, Amrita, 'All That Glitters Is Not Gold: India's Rise to Power', *Third World Quarterly*, vol. 28, no. 5 (2007), pp. 983–996.

Narlikar, Amrita, 'India Rising: Responsible to Whom?' *International Affairs*, vol. 89, no. 3 (2013), pp. 595–614.

Nayar, Baldev Raj and T. V. Paul, *India in the World Order: Searching for Major Power Status* (Cambridge: Cambridge University Press, 2003).

Nayyar, Deepak, 'Economic Growth in Independent India: Lumbering Elephant or Running Tiger?' *Economic and Political Weekly*, vol. 41, no. 15 (April 15–21 2006), pp. 1451–1458.

Nehru, Jawaharlal, *The Discovery of India*, New Delhi: Penguin (2004 [1946]).

Nehru, Jawaharlal, *Letters to Chief Ministers, vol. 1, 1947–1949* (Oxford: Oxford University Press, 1990).

Nehru, Jawaharlal, 'Free India's Role in World Affairs', in Jawaharlal Nehru, *Selected Works of Jawaharlal Nehru: Second Series*, vol. I (New Delhi: Oxford University Press, 1984).

Nehru, Jawaharlal, *Speeches, Volume 1: 1946–1949* (New Delhi: Ministry of Information and Broadcasting, 1967)

Nehru, Jawaharlal, *Speeches. Volume 2: 1949–1953* (Delhi: Ministry of Information and Broadcasting, 1954).

Nehru, Jawaharlal, 'Speech to the US Congress', 13 October 1949, www.rediff.com/news/report/nehru-was-the-first-pm-to-address-the-us-congress/20160601.htm (accessed on 5 November 2016).

Nesadurai, Helen E. S., 'Bandung and the Political Economy of North–South Relations: Sowing the Seeds for Re-visioning International Society', in See Seng Tan and Amitav Acharya, eds, *Bandung Revisited: The Legacy of the Asian-African Conference for International Order* (Singapore: NUS Press, 2008), pp. 68–101.

Neumann, Iver B., and Benjamin de Carvalho, 'Introduction: Small States and Status', in Benjamin de Carvalho and Iver B. Neumann, eds, *A Great Power*

Performance: Norway's Quest for Higher Standing (Abingdon and New York: Routledge, 2015), pp. 56–72.

Neumann, Iver B., 'Status is Cultural: Durkheimian Poles and Weberian Russians Seek Great Power Status', in T. V. Paul, Deborah Welch Larson and William C. Wohlforth, eds, *Status in World Politics* (New York: Cambridge University Press, 2014), pp. 85–112.

'Non-Proliferation Humbug', *Economic and Political Weekly*, vol. 3, no. 11 (16 March 1968), p. 441.

Norris, Robert S. and Hans M. Kristensen, 'Global Nuclear Inventories, 1945–2013', *Bulletin of the Atomic Scientists*, vol. 69, no. 5 (2013), pp. 75–81.

Ogden, Chris, *Hindu Nationalism and the Evolution of Contemporary Indian Security* (New Delhi: Oxford University Press, 2014).

Panda, Ankit, 'Why Does India Have So Many "Strategic Partners" and No Allies?' *The Diplomat*, 23 November 2013, http://thediplomat.com/2013/11/why-does-india-have-so-many-strategic-partners-and-no-allies/ (accessed on 2 December 2016).

Panikkar, K. M., *India and the Indian Ocean: An Essay on the Influence of Sea Power on Indian History* (London: Macmillan, 1945).

Pant, Harsh V., 'A Rising India's Search for a Foreign Policy', *Orbis*, vol. 53, no. 2 (2009), pp. 250–264.

Pant, Harsh V., *Contemporary Debates in Indian Foreign and Security Policy* (Basingstoke: Palgrave Macmillan, 2012).

Parameswaran, Prashanth, 'Return of Asia's Quad "Natural": US Defense Chief', *The Diplomat*, 9 April 2016, http://thediplomat.com/2016/04/return-of-asias-quad-natural-us-defense-chief/ (accessed on 22 November 2016).

Parameswaran, Prashanth, 'Explaining US Strategic Partnerships in the Asia-Pacific Region: Origins, Development and Prospects', *Contemporary Southeast Asia*, vol. 36, no. 2 (2014), pp. 262–289.

Pardesi, Manjeet S., 'Understanding the Rise of India', *India Review*, vol. 6, no. 3 (2007), pp. 209–231.

Parekh, Bhikhu, 'Nehru and the National Philosophy of India', *Economic and Political Weekly* (5 January 1991), pp. 35–48.

Paul, T. V., ed., *Accommodating Rising Powers: Past, Present and Future* (New York: Cambridge University Press, 2016).

Paul, T. V. and Mahesh Shankar, 'Status Accommodation through Institutional Means: India's Rise in the Global Order', in T. V. Paul, Deborah Welch Larson and William C. Wohlforth, eds, *Status in World Politics* (New York: Cambridge University Press, 2014), pp. 165–191.

Parayil, Govindan, 'The Green Revolution in India: A Case Study of Technological Change', *Technology and Culture*, vol. 33, no. 4 (1992), pp. 737–756.

Perkovich, George, *India's Nuclear Bomb: The Impact on Global Proliferation* (New Delhi: Oxford University Press, 2002).

Piccone, Ted, *Five Rising Democracies and the Fate of the International Liberal Order* (Washington, DC: Brookings Institution Press, 2016).

Poddar, Tushar and Eva Yi, 'India's Rising Growth Potential', Economics Paper no. 152, Goldman Sachs, January 2007.

Rajagopalan, Rajeswari Pillai and Arka Biswas, *Wassenaar Arrangement: The Case of India's Membership*, Observer Research Foundation, New Delhi, May 2016, http://cf.orfonline.org/wp-content/uploads/2016/05/ORF-Occasional-Paper_92.pdf (accessed on 20 November 2016).

Rajan, M. S., 'The Non-Aligned Movement: The New Delhi Conference and After', *Southeast Asian Affairs* (1 January 1982), pp. 60–72.

Rajan, M. S., 'India: A Case of Power without Force', *International Journal*, vol. 30, no. 2 (1995), pp. 299–325.

Rajan, Mukund Govind, *Global Environmental Politics: India and the North–South Politics of Global Environmental Issues* (Delhi: Oxford University Press, 1997).

Ramesh, Jairam, *To the Brink and Back: India's 1991 Story* (New Delhi: Rupa, 2015).

Ravenhill, John, 'The North–South Balance of Power', *International Affairs*, vol. 6, no. 4 (1990), pp. 731–748.

Ray, Jayanta Kumar, *India's Foreign Relations, 1947–2007* (New Delhi: Routledge, 2011), ch. 10.

'RBI's Gold Buying Has Its Own Sentimental Value: FM', *Outlook* (3 November 2009) www.outlookindia.com/newswire/story/rbis-gold-buying-has-its-own-sentimental-value-fm/668864/?next (accessed on 18 November 2016).

Reid, Anthony, 'The Bandung Conference and Southeast Asian Regionalism', in See Seng Tan and Amitav Acharaya, eds, *Bandung Revisited: The Legacy of the Asian-African Conference for International Order* (Singapore: NUS Press, 2008), pp. 19–26.

'Remarks of Secretary of State Condoleezza Rice at the Senate Foreign Relations Committee on the US–India Civil Nuclear Cooperation Initiative', 5 April 2006, www.globalsecurity.org/wmd/library/congress/2006_h/060405-rice.pdf (accessed on 20 November 2016).

Renard, Thomas, 'The EU Strategic Partnerships Review: Ten Guiding Principles', Policy Brief #2 (2012), European Strategic Partnerships Observatory, Brussels, www.ies.be/files/private/28%29%20Renard%20-%20Ten%20Guiding%20Principles.pdf (accessed on 10 February 2015).

Reus-Smit, Christian, 'Reading History through Constructivist Eyes', *Millennium: Journal of International Studies*, vol. 37, no. 2 (2008), pp. 395–414.

Rosenau, James N., *The Study of Global Interdependence: Essays on the Transnationalization of World Affairs* (London: Frances Pinter, 1980).

Rout, Hemant Kumar, 'Stage Set for Longer-Range Surya', *New Indian Express*, 18 September 2013, www.newindianexpress.com/states/odisha/Stage-set-for-longer-range-Surya/2013/09/18/article1790125.ece (accessed 22 February 2015).

Rubinoff, Arthur G., 'The Multilateral Imperative in India's Foreign Policy', *The Round Table*, no. 319 (1991), pp. 313–334.

Rudolph, Lloyd I. and Susanne Hoeber Rudolph, *The Modernity of Tradition: Political Development in India* (Chicago and London: University of Chicago Press, 1967).

Rudolph, Susanne Hoeber and Lloyd I. Rudolph, 'New Dimensions in Indian Democracy', *Journal of Democracy*, vol. 13, no. 1 (2002), pp. 52–66.

Sagan, Scott D., 'Why Do States Build Nuclear Weapons? Three Models in Search of a Bomb', *International Security*, vol. 21, no. 3 (1996–1997), pp. 54–86.

Saksena, Jyotika, 'Regime Design Matters: The CTBT and India's Nuclear Dilemma', *Comparative Strategy*, vol. 25, no. 3 (July 2006), pp. 209–229.

Sasikumar, Karthika, 'India's Emergence as a Responsible Nuclear Power', *International Journal*, vol. 62, no. 4 (2007), pp. 825–844.

Schaffer, Howard B. and Teresita C. Schaffer, *India at the Global High Table: The Quest for Regional Primacy and Strategic Autonomy* (Washington, DC: Brookings Institution Press, 2016).

Schaffer, Teresita and Joan Rohlfing, *India and the Non-Proliferation System: A Report of the Working Group on an Expanded Non-proliferation System*, Nuclear Threat Initiative, Washington, DC, November 2011, www.nti.org/media/pdfs/IndiaNonProliferationSystem-1111.pdf?_=1326131244 (accessed on 20 November 2016).

Schirm, Stefan A., 'Leaders in Need of Followers: Emerging Powers in Global Governance', *European Journal of International Relations*, vol. 16, no. 2 (June 2010), pp. 197–221.

Sen, Sunanda, 'New International Economic Order and Contemporary World Economic Scene', *Economic and Political Weekly*, vol. 16, no. 10/12 (March 1981), pp. 516–525.

Sibal, Kanwal, '"Strategic" Relations Suit India', *Mail Today*, 26 December 2012, http://indiatoday.in/story/strategic-relations-suit-india-india-today/1/239437.html (accessed on 3 February 2015).

Sibal, Rajeev, 'The Untold Story of India's Economy', in Nicholas Kitchen, ed., *India: The Next Superpower* (London: London School of Economics, 2012), pp. 17–22.

Sidhu, Waheguru Pal Singh, Pratap Bhanu Mehta and Bruce Jones, eds, *Shaping the Emerging World: India and the Multilateral Order* (Washington, DC: Brookings Institution Press, 2013).

Siisiäinen, Martti, 'Two Concepts of Social Capital: Bourdieu vs. Putnam', Paper presented at ISTR Fourth International Conference on 'The Third Sector: For What and for Whom?'Trinity College, Dublin, Ireland, 5–8 July 2000, http://c.ymcdn.com/sites/www.istr.org/resource/resmgr/working_papers_dublin/siisiainen.pdf (accessed on 22 February 2015).

Silva, Marina Magalhães Barreto Leite, 'Spoiler or Reformer? The Uniting for Consensus Group and Security Council Reform', Ph.D. dissertation, Osaka University, January 2014, http://ir.library.osaka-u.ac.jp/dspace/bitstream/11094/34548/1/26639_%E8%AB%96%E6%96%87.pdf (accessed on 20 November 2016).

Singham, A. W. and Shirley Hune, *Non-alignment in an Age of Alignments* (London: Zed Books).

Singh, Abhijit, 'The Indian Ocean Zone of Peace: Reality vs. Illusion', *The Diplomat*, 7 January 2015, http://thediplomat.com/2015/01/the-indian-ocea n-zone- of-peace-reality-vs-illusion/ (accessed on 8 December 2016).

Singh, Jaswant, *In Service of Emergent India: A Call to Honour* (Bloomington and Indianapolis: Indiana University Press, 2007).

Singh, K.Natwar, 'The Seventh Non-Aligned Summit, New Delhi, March 1983', *The Round Table*, no. 287 (1983), pp. 328–330.

Singh, Manmohan, 'PM's Valedictory Address to the Fifth Session of the 14th Lok Sabha', 30 August 2005, http://archivepmo.nic.in/drmanmohansingh/sp eech-details.php?nodeid=172 (accessed on 5 December 2016).

Srinivas, M. N., *Social Change in Modern India* (Hyderabad: Orient Black Swan, 1966).

Stockholm International Peace Research Institute, 'SIPRI Military Expendi- ture Database: Military Expenditure Data 1949–2015' (2016), https://www. sipri.org/databases/milex (accessed on 10 September 2016).

Stockholm International Peace Research Institute, *SIPRI Yearbook 2015* (Oxford: Oxford University Press, 2015).

Sullivan, Kate, *The Evolution of India's Great Power Identity: A Powerful Performance*, PhD Dissertation, The Australian National University, Australia (April 2011).

Sullivan, Kate, 'Exceptionalism in Indian Diplomacy: The Origins of India's Moral Leadership Aspirations', *South Asia: Journal of South Asian Studies*, vol. 37, no. 4 (2014), pp.640–655.

Sullivan, Kate, *Is India a Responsible Nuclear Power?* Policy report, S. Rajar- atnam School of International Studies, Nanyang Technological University, Singapore, March 2014.

Sullivan, Kate, ed., *Competing Visions of India in World Politics: India's Rise Beyond the West* (Basingstoke: Palgrave Macmillan, 2015).

Sullivan, Kate, 'India's Ambivalent Projection of Self as a Global Power: Between Compliance and Resistance', in Kate Sullivan, ed., *Competing Visions of India in World Politics* (Basingstoke: Palgrave Macmillan, 2015), pp. 15–33.

Sullivan de Estrada, Kate, 'India and UN Security Council Reform 1990–1997', Unpublished paper (2016).

Sullivan de Estrada, Kate and Nicholas J. Wheeler, 'Trustworthy Nuclear Sovereigns? India and Pakistan after the 1998 Tests', *Stosunki Międzynar- odowe – International Relations*, vol. 52, no. 2 (2016). doi: 10.7366/ 020909612201614.

Sullivan de Estrada, Kate and Patrick Quinton-Brown, 'The Myth of India's Non-Aligned Boycott', *The Diplomat* (23 November 2016), http://thedip lomat.com/2016/11/the-myth-of-indias-non-aligned-boycott/ (accessed 6 December 2016).

Swami, Praveen, 'Upset with Delay, Kabul Shelves Request for Arms Aid from Delhi', *Indian Express*, 30 October 2014, http://indianexpress.com/article/ india/india-others/upset-with-delay-kabul-shelves-request-for-arms-aid-from- delhi/ (accessed on 22 February 2015).

Swart, Lydia, 'Reform of the Security Council: 2007–2013', in United Nations, *Governing and Managing Change at the United Nations*, vol. 1 (New York: Center for UN Reform Education, September 2013), pp. 23–60.

'Taliban Praise India for Resisting Afghan Entanglement', *Express Tribune*, 17 June 2002, http://tribune.com.pk/story/395024/taliban-praise-india-for-resisting-afghan-entanglement/ (accessed on 22 February 2015).

Tan, See Seng and Amitav Acharya, eds, *Bandung Revisited: The Legacy of the Asian-African Conference for International Order* (Singapore: NUS Press, 2008).

'Text of the Indo–Soviet Treaty', *Mainstream*, 13 August 2011, https://www.ma instreamweekly.net/article2950.html (accessed on 27 November 2016).

Tharoor, Shashi, *Reasons of State: Political Development and India's Foreign Policy under Indira Gandhi, 1966–1977* (New Delhi: Vikas, 1982).

Tiwari, Ravish, 'BJP Calls for a Muscular Foreign Policy: Panchamrit to Replace Panchsheel', *India Today*, 4 April 2016, http://indiatoday.intoday.in/story/bjp-foreign-policy-national-executive/1/428383.html (accessed on 20 May 2016).

Tyabji, Badr-ud-din, *Memoirs of an Egoist, Volume One: 1907–1956* (New Delhi: Roli, 1988).

United Nations, Doc. A/C.1/L.239 and Add.1.

United Nations, Doc. DC/98 31 July 1956.

United Nations, *The United Nations and Disarmament 1945–70* (New York: United Nations, 1970).

United States, Department of State, 'Hearing on U.S.–India Civil Nuclear Cooperation Initiative: R. Nicholas Burns, Under Secretary for Political Affairs, Remarks as Prepared for the Senate Foreign Relations Committee', 2 November 2005, https://2001-2009.state.gov/p/us/rm/2005/55969.htm (accessed on 21 November 2016).

United States, Department of State, 'Background Briefing by Administration Officials on US–South Asia Relations', 25 March 2005, https://2001-2009.sta te.gov/r/pa/prs/ps/2005/43853.htm (accessed on 20 November 2016).

United States Senate, Committee on Environment and Public Works, 'Hearing Statements', 16 June 2006, www.epw.senate.gov/hearing_statements.cfm?id= 257222 (accessed on 21 November 2016).

United States, White House, Office of the Press Secretary, 'Joint Statement between President George W. Bush and Prime Minister Manmohan Singh', 18 July 2005, http://georgewbushwhitehouse.archives.gov/news/releases/2005/07/20050718-6.html (accessed on 21 November 2016).

Varshney, Ashutosh, 'Mass Politics or Elite Politics? India's Economic Reforms in Comparative Perspective', *Journal of Policy Reform*, vol. 2, no. 4 (1998), pp. 301–335.

Varshney, Ashutosh, *Battles Half Won: India's Improbable Democracy* (New Delhi: Penguin, 2013).

Volgy, Thomas J., Renato Corbetta, J. Patrick Rhamey Jr, Ryan G. Baird and Keith A. Grant, 'Status Considerations in International Politics and the Rise of Regional Powers', in T. V. Paul, Deborah Welch Larson and William C. Wohlforth, eds, *Status in World Politics* (New York: Cambridge University Press, 2014), pp. 58–84.

Volgy, Thomas J., Renato Corbetta, Keith A. Grant and Ryan G. Baird, eds, *Major Powers and the Quest for Status in International Politics: Global and Regional Perspectives* (New York: Palgrave, 2011).

Wheeler, Nicholas J., *Saving Strangers: Humanitarian Intervention in International Society* (Oxford: Oxford University Press, 2000).

Widmark, Otto, 'India's Aspiration for a Permanent Membership at the Security Council: An Update', Issue brief, Delhi Policy Group, New Delhi, January 2015.

Wilkins, Thomas S., '"Alignment", not "Alliance" – the Shifting Paradigm of International Security Cooperation: Toward a Conceptual Taxonomy of Alignment', *Review of International Studies*, vol. 38, no. 1 (2012), pp. 53–76.

Willetts, Peter, *The Non-Aligned Movement: The Origins of a Third World Alliance* (London: Frances Pinter, 1978).

Wilson, Lou and Peter Mayer, 'Upward Mobility and Social Capital: Building Advantage through Volunteering', Australian Policy Online, 16 January 2007, http://apo.org.au/research/upward-mobility-and-social-capital-building-advantage-through-volunteering (accessed on 22 February 2015).

Wolf Jr, Charles, Gregory Hildebrandt, Michael Kennedy, Donald Putnam Henry, Katsuaki Terasawa, K. C. Yeh, Benjamin Zycher, Anil Bamezai and Toshiya Hayashi, *Long-Term Economic and Military Trends 1950–2010: A Rand Note* (Santa Monica, CA: Rand Corporation, April 1989).

World Bank, 'World Bank National Accounts Data, and OECD National Accounts Data Files', http://data.worldbank.org/indicator/NE.TRD.GNFS.ZS?end=1990&start=1964 (accessed on 26 November 2016).

World ResourcesInstitute, 'Top 10 Emitters in 2012', May 2016, www.wri.org/resources/charts-graphs/top-10-emitters-2012 (accessed on 11 December 2016).

Zakaria, Fareed, 'India Rising', *Newsweek*, 5 March 2006, www.newsweek.com/india-rising-106259 (accessed on 2 February 2015).

Zakaria, Fareed, 'Interview with Narendra Modi; Interview with Bill Clinton', *Global Public Square*, broadcast 21 September 2014, transcript available at: http://edition.cnn.com/TRANSCRIPTS/1409/21/fzgps.01.html (accessed on 3 December 2016).

Zhongping, Feng and Huang Jing, 'China's Strategic Partnership Diplomacy: Engaging with a Changing World', Working paper #8 (June 2014), European Strategic Partnerships Observatory, Brussels, http://strategicpartnerships.eu/publications/chinas-strategic-partnership-diplomacy-engaging-with-a-changing-world/ (accessed on 10 February 2015).

Index

Note: 'N' after a page number indicates a note; 'f' indicates a figure; 't' indicates a table.

Afghanistan 101
Afro-Asian Group 40, 42
Alberuni 1
Anthony, A. K. 92
Arab-Asian Group 40
ARC *see* Asian Relations Conference (ARC)
Arunachalam, V. S. 60, 61
Asian Relations Conference (ARC) 39
Asia Pacific Economic Cooperation (APEC) 89
associations: Milner's view of 5–6; of Nehru era 24, 26–37; in post-Cold War period 86–93; of post-Nehru era 28–34, 55–56; as source of status 11; *see also* non-alignment policy

Bajpai, G. S. 31, 47, 59
Bandung Conference (1955) 41–42
Basrur, Rajesh 7
Belgrade conference 43
Bhabha, Homi 32
Bharatiya Janata Party (BJP) 102
Blackett, P. M. S. 29
Blackwill, Robert 99
Bowles, Chester 48
Brecher, Michael 37
Brennan, Geoffrey 8
Burawoy, Michael 13
Burns, R. Nicholas 99

Bush, George W. 91, 98, 99
Buzan, Barry 27

capitalism: in Nehru era 46–48; in post-Cold War period 98–100; in post-Nehru era 74–75
case studies, defined 12–13
Chagla, M. C. 60, 71
Chari, P. R. 36–37, 58
China: and nuclear testing 60; and Sino-Indian War (1962) 31; status of 5; status of, vs. India 6
climate change *see* environmental issues
Clunan, Anne 12
Cohen, Stephen 87, 88
Cold War, and nuclear weapons race 26, 55
Conference of Oppressed Nationalities 39
conformity: as normative source of status 11; as status-seeking strategy 8; *see also* norms
consistency *see* status consistency/inconsistency
'counter-order' strategies: of Nehru era 37, 38–41, 44; in post-Nehru era 54–55, 63–70; *see also* creativity/innovation
creativity/innovation: and Indian status 11–12; of non-alignment policy 37–38; as normative source

of status 11, 17–18; as status-seeking strategy 8; success of, as status-seeking strategy 18; *see also* 'counter-order' strategies
Cuba 67

Dasgupta, Sunil 87, 88
Dayal, Rajeshwar 40, 42
de Carvalho, Benjamin 103
democracy: in Nehru era 24, 46–48, 113; in post-Cold War period 98–100; in post-Nehru era 74–75
Deng, Yong 5, 7
Desai, Morarji 73, 74
Deshmukh, B. G. 70
deviance *see* resistance/deviance
disarmament *see* non-proliferation
Disarmament Commission 45, 46

economic power: of Nehru era 28–29; in post-Cold War period 83, 84, 85, 86–87, 100; in post-Nehru era 55–56, 57–58, 75; as status determinant 12
Efstathopoulos, Charalampos 95
Eighteen Nation Disarmament Committee (ENDC) 71
ENDC *see* Eighteen Nation Disarmament Committee (ENDC)
environmental issues 66–67, 95–96
esteem, defined 8

food shortages 57
Fukuryu Maru incident (1954) 45

Gandhi, Indira 3; and corrupt electoral practices 74, 114; on economic policies 61–62; on environmental issues 66–67; on foreign policy 69; as leader in post-Nehru era 57; on material power 59; on nuclear energy 72; and nuclear weapons 60–61; on Pakistan 69
Gandhi, Rajiv 60, 61, 70, 73
Ganguly, Sumit 57
Gayoom, Abdul 70
Geneva Conference (1954) 41
Gerring, John 12

'good power': concept of 5; India as 6
Gopal, Sarvepalli 43
Great Britain 5
'green revolution' 61
Group of 20 (G20) 89
Group of 77 (G77) 56, 75, 76
Group of Four (G4) 92
Gupta, Sisir 71

humanitarian assistance 101
human rights protection 85–86, 96

ICC *see* International Criminal Court (ICC)
inconsistency *see* status consistency/inconsistency
India: as 'good power' 6; moral leadership of, during Nehru era 25, 31, 33; previous studies of, relevant to status 9–10; status of, vs. China 6; *see also* Nehru era (1947–1964); post-Cold War period (1991-present); post-Nehru era (1964–1991)
Indo-Soviet Treaty of Peace, Friendship and Cooperation (1971) 62
innovation *see* creativity/innovation
International Criminal Court (ICC) 5
International Monetary Fund (IMF) 83
Iran 23n62

Jakarta Summit 94
Japan 5, 91, 92
Jha, Chandra Shekhar 64, 71
Johnson, Lyndon 61

Kashmir dispute 35–36, 38
Keenleyside, T. A. 34
Keohane, Robert 8
Khan, Ayub 64
Kissinger, Henry 60
Kyoto Protocol 5

Lall, Arthur Samuel 46, 59
Larson, Deborah Welch 4–5, 8, 10
Lebow, Richard Ned 5, 11, 22n50
Lugar, Richard 99

material power: Indira Gandhi on 59;
in Nehru era 24, 29–32, 113; in
post-Cold War period 84–86, 115;
in post-Nehru era 56–57, 114;
realist tradition's view of 2–3; shift
toward, from non-material status
seeking 2; as status determinant 4,
12; status seeking delinked from 3;
status seeking linked to 3; *see also*
military power
McCartney, Matthew 57–58
Menon, V. K. Krishna 32, 46
methodology of study 12–15
military power: after Sino-Indian
War (1962) 36–37; Lebow on
22n50; of Nehru era 29–32; in
post-Cold War period 85–86,
87–88, 100–103; in post-Nehru era
54, 57, 58–59, 69–70; as status
enhancing 11; *see also* material
power; nuclear weapons
Milner, Murray 5, 10, 11, 112
Missile Technology Control Regime
(MTCR) 97
Modi, Narendra 15, 94, 100,
102–103; on India as "golden
bird" 1
moral leadership: of India during
Nehru era 25, 31; and Kashmir
dispute 35–36, 38; and nuclear
energy 33
Morgenthau, Hans 19–20n9
MTCR *see* Missile Technology
Control Regime (MTCR)
Mukherjee, Rahul 57
Mukherjee, Rohan 8

NAM *see* Non-Aligned Movement
(NAM)
Nandy, Ashis 72
Nayar, Baldev Raj 7, 9–10
negative status, deviance as source of 11
Nehru, Jawaharlal: at Bandung
Conference (1955) 41–42; and
Belgrade conference 43; on India
as "great power" 1; on India's
international role 39–40; on non-
alignment policy 35; on nuclear
energy 33–34; on nuclear
weapons 44

Nehru era (1947–1964): associational
status seeking during 28–34;
associations during 26–28; and
capitalism 46–48; 'counter-order'
strategies of 37, 38–41, 44; and
democracy 24, 46–48, 113;
economic power during 28–29;
innovation as source of status
during 11–12, 17–18, 24; material
power in 113; military power
during 29–32; moral leadership of
India during 25, 31, 33; Non-
Aligned Movement (NAM) 113;
non-alignment policy during 30;
non-proliferation as normative
source of status 44–46; normative
status seeking during 26–28,
37–48; nuclear weapons as rejected
during 24–25, 32–34; overview of
14, 16; overview of status-seeking
during 24–26; and relations with
dominant powers 34–37; and
Sino-Indian War (1962) 31, 32, 36,
113; Soviet relations during 36, 37;
status seeking delinked to material
power 3; U.S. relations during
27–28, 29, 34, 36, 37, 47
Neumann, Iver 101, 103
New Delhi Declaration 68
New International Economic Order
(NIEO) 65
NIEO *see* New International
Economic Order (NIEO)
Nixon, Richard 69
Non-Aligned Movement (NAM)
43, 54, 56, 62, 63–66, 67–68,
93–95, 113
non-alignment policy: abandonment
of 37; as innovative status-seeking
strategy 37–38; of Nehru era 30,
34–37; Nehru on 35; of post-
Nehru era 62, 63; and Sino-Indian
War (1962) 36; *see also*
associations
non-proliferation: as emerging
norm 25, 56; in Nehru era 44–46;
in post-Cold War period 96–98;
in post-Nehru era 70–74; *see also*
Nuclear Non-Proliferation
Treaty (NPT)

norms: and democracy 46–48; of Nehru era 24, 26–28; and Nehru-era status seeking 37–48; in post-Cold War period 84–86; and post-Cold War status seeking 93–103; of post-Nehru era 55–56; and post-Nehru status seeking 63–75; as status determinant 4–6, 11; *see also* conformity

North Atlantic Treaty Organisation (NATO) 93

Norway 5

NPT *see* Nuclear Non-Proliferation Treaty (NPT)

NSG *see* Nuclear Suppliers Group (NSG)

nuclear energy 32–34, 72

Nuclear Non-Proliferation Treaty (NPT) 46, 55, 56, 60, 71–72, 97; *see also* non-proliferation

Nuclear Suppliers Group (NSG) 6, 96–97, 116

nuclear weapons: and Cold War build-up 26, 55; and Indian status-seeking 3; Nehru-era rejection of 24–25, 32–34; Nehru on 44; 'Peaceful Nuclear Explosion' (1974) 72–73; in post-Cold War period 83–84, 88; in post-Nehru era 55, 57, 59–61; and sanctions against India 73; *see also* military power; non-proliferation

oil crisis (1973) 57

OPEC *see* Organisation of Petroleum Exporting Countries (OPEC)

'Operation Cactus' (1988) 70

Organisation of Petroleum Exporting Countries (OPEC) 65

Pakistan 69

panchsheel 31, 50n40

Panikkar, K. M. 31

Paris Accord (2015) 96

Patel, Sardar Vallabhbhai 31

Paul, T. V. 4–5, 7, 9–10

'Peaceful Nuclear Explosion' (1974) 72–73

Pettit, Philip 8

piracy 101

post-Cold War period (1991-present) 96; associational status seeking during 86–93; and capitalism 98–100; and democracy 98–100; economic power in 83, 84, 85, 86–87, 100; and environmental issues 95–96; human rights protection in 85–86, 96; material power in 3, 84–86, 115; military power in 85–86, 87–88, 100–103; multilateral groupings 91; Non-Aligned Movement (NAM) 83, 93–95; non-proliferation in 96–98; normative status seeking during 93–103; norms during 84–86; nuclear weapons in 83–84, 88; overview of 14, 16–17; and relations with dominant powers 89–93; shift in status-seeking strategies during 82–84; use of force in 100–103; U.S. relations during 88, 89, 90, 91, 97, 99

post-Nehru era (1964–1991): associational status seeking during 56–63; associations during 55–56; and capitalism 74–75; 'counter-order' strategies of 54–55, 63–70; and democracy 74–75; economic policies of 61–62; economic power in 55–56, 57–58, 75; and environmental issues 66–67; material power in 56–57, 114; military power in 54, 57, 58–59, 69–70; and Non-Aligned Movement (NAM) 63–66, 67–68; non-alignment policy 62, 63; non-proliferation in 70–74; normative status seeking during 63–75; norms during 55–56; and Nuclear Non-Proliferation Treaty (NPT) 60; nuclear weapons in 55, 57, 59–61, 70–74; overview of 14, 16; overview of status-seeking during 54–55; and relations with dominant powers 61–63; Soviet relations during 58–59, 62

Prasad, Rajendra 30, 31

prestige 19–20n9; defined 2

Rao, P. V. Narasimha 68, 83, 86, 94
realist tradition, on material power
   and status 2–3
rejection, as status-seeking strategy 8
resistance/deviance, as normative
   source of status 11
responsibility, and 'status
   enactment' 12
'Responsibility to Protect' (R2P) 84,
   86, 96
Rice, Condoleezza 88, 99
Romulo, Carlos 42

Shastri, Lal Bahadur 60
Shevchenko, Alexei 8
'short tether' policy 61
Singh, Charan 74
Singh, K. Natwar 68
Singh, Manmohan 83, 86, 90, 98, 100
Sino-Indian War (1962) 31, 32, 36,
   56, 58, 59, 113
social capital, defined 9
social construction, status as 10,
   22n48
Soviet Union: Nehru-era associations
   with 36; and Non-Aligned
   Movement (NAM) 67–68; and
   post-Nehru relations 58–59, 62;
   see also 'superpowers'
Sri Lanka 70, 101, 102
START *see* Strategic Arms
   Reduction Treaty (START)
status: defined 2, 10–12; vs. esteem 8;
   as linked to material power 3; as
   power resource 8–9; previous
   studies of, relevant to India 9–10;
   realist tradition's view of 2–3; as
   socially constructed 10, 22n48;
   successful strategies for obtaining
   18; *see also* negative status
status accommodation 6–7
status consistency/inconsistency 7
status determinants: associational
   5–6, 11; economic power 12;
   material power as 4, 12; normative
   4–6, 11; status accommodation
   6–7
'status enactment' 12, 100–103

status-seeking behaviours,
   identification of 14–15
status-seeking strategies: conformity
   8; delinked from material power 3;
   Larson and Shevchenko's
   categories 8; Lebow's classification
   of 7–8; Mukherjee's categories 8;
   rejection 8; shift from non-material
   to material power 2; study
   methodology 12–15; *see also*
   specific strategies
Strategic Arms Reduction Treaty
   (START) 85
Subterranean Nuclear Explosion
   Project 60
'superpowers': and Nehru-era
   non-alignment policy 24, 34–37;
   post-Cold War relations with
   89–93; post-Nehru relations with
   61–63; *see also* Soviet Union;
   United States

Trivedi, V. C. 71

UNCTAD *see* United Nations
   Conference on Trade and
   Development (UNCTAD)
United Nations 40, 45
United Nations Conference on
   Trade and Development
   (UNCTAD) 65, 66
United Nations Security Council
   (UNSC) 6, 92
United States: and Nehru-era
   relations 27–28, 29, 34, 36, 47;
   and post-Cold War relations 88,
   89, 90, 91, 97, 99; and post-Nehru
   relations 61, 62; *see also*
   'superpowers'
UNSC *see* United Nations Security
   Council (UNSC)

Wassenaar Arrangement 97
Wohlforth, William C. 4–5
World Trade Organisation 89, 95

Zakaria, Fareed 100
Zhou Enlai 41

For Product Safety Concerns and Information please contact our EU
representative GPSR@taylorandfrancis.com
Taylor & Francis Verlag GmbH, Kaufingerstraße 24, 80331 München, Germany

www.ingramcontent.com/pod-product-compliance
Ingram Content Group UK Ltd.
Pitfield, Milton Keynes, MK11 3LW, UK
UKHW021838240425
457818UK00007B/225